REFERENCE GUIDE FOR PHARMACY MANAGEMENT & PHARMACOECONOMICS

2018 – 2019 EDITION

MANAN SHROFF

This reference guide is not intended as a substitute for the advice of a physician. Students or readers must consult their physician about any existing problem. Do not use any information of this reference guide for any kind of self-treatment. Do not administer any dose of mentioned drugs in this reference guide without consulting your physician. This is only a review guide for the preparation of the Foreign Pharmacy Licensing Exam (FPGEE®), and North American Pharmacy Licensing Exam (NAPLEX®)

The author of this reference guide is not responsible for any kind of misinterpreted, incorrect or misleading information or any typographical errors in this guide. Any doubtful or questionable answers should be checked in other available reference sources.

PREFACE:

I am very happy to introduce this new edition that covers the major portion of pharmacy management and pharmacoeconomics. As in recent years, FPGEE exam is putting more weight on management and the economic portion of the pharmaceutical field, which has inspired me to introduce a guide that may help students to answers questions in the exam related to these topics.

I tried to cover all the pharmacy management and pharmacoeconomics aspects in this guide. The reason to introduce this review guide is to provide foreign students with enough information regarding the management aspect of health care in the U.S.

The students must try to understand the information provided in this guide since that's the only way to apply your logic to answer management and economics related questions in the exam. You may not receive straightforward questions from this guide, however the information presented in this guide will definitely help you to guess the best logical answer for a given question.

I hope my efforts will bring you much success.

Best of luck,

Manan H. Shroff

Table of Contents

SOCIAL AND BEHAVIORAL ASPECT OF PHARMACEUTICAL CARE

1. Social and Behavioral Aspect of Pharmaceutical Care

Pharmaceutical Care: It is the study of the logical consequences of the evolution of the profession of the pharmacy.

What is the true meaning of health?

It is a very hard task to define health since it is not limited to a single factor. For example, if we try to define health by using medical definition, it would not be sufficient since there are sociological, epidemiological, health planning and physiological definitions as well. In short, it is hard to define health by using a single factor. In medical terms, health may be defined as the absence of disease or the maintenance of physiological parameters within accepted norms (e.g. blood glucose, blood pressure, cholesterol).

Anderson has summarized epidemiological and health planning definitions into five major categories. These are:

1. Health as a product or outcome (the result of adequate planning and utilization of resources).
2. Health as a potential or capacity to achieve goals.
3. Health as an everchanging dynamic process (the interaction between agent, host, and environment).
4. Health as something experienced by individuals.
5. Health as an attribute of an individual.

According to the World Health Organization, health is the state of complete physical, mental, and social well-being, and not merely the absence of disease or infirmity.

The Quality of Pharmaceutical Care: The quality of pharmaceutical care can be evaluated and examined by resources such as structure, process, and outcome components.

A. **Structure Resources**: Structure resources are required to obtain high-level quality care. For example, one must have laminar flow hood in order to provide the highest quality of parenterals admixtures. It does not matter how efficient or smart you are, structural resources play an important role to address the quality of care. Referring to the above example, obviously if you have a home-infusion company without laminar flow hood, the quality of parenteral preparations will be considered poor. Therefore, the structural resources would be considered necessary to obtain a high level of quality care.

B. **Process Resources**: It refers to many activities performed by a pharmacist that are considered a part of quality care. Referring to the parenteral preparation example; the use of aseptic technique while making IV admixtures is defined as a process resource.

C. **Outcomes**: It refers to the experience of a patient who receives the care. The high quality of care is assumed when the patient experiences the desirable outcomes. Thus, the structure, process, and outcomes are intended to be part of an integrated model of quality care assessment. Another example that explains the quality of care is a hospital with a CAT scanner is presumed to render a higher quality of care than a hospital without one.

2. Health Behavior

Health behavior is an action taken by a healthy person for the purpose of remaining healthy or in an asymptomatic state. For example, brushing teeth, avoiding tobacco and alcohol, regular exercising, wearing a seat belt, etc. People engage in such behaviors for several reasons, including habit, attraction, fear or death.

A Model of Health Behavior or Health Belief Model

The Health Belief Model was developed to give healthcare professions an idea as to why and under what conditions people take preventive health actions or behaviors. The Health Belief Model depends on three classes of variables:

1. The individual's psychological state of readiness to take specific action.

2. The degree to which a particular course of action is believed to have a net beneficial effect in reducing the health threat.

3. A cure to action that may trigger appropriate action when needed.

Christensen, Fincham and Wertheimer have used the Health Belief Model to find out the patients' compliance with therapeutic regimens. Christensen also proposed that compliance with the drug therapy is a dynamic process in which patients continuously reassess the decision to comply.

Fincham and Wertheimer used the Health Belief Model to predict the patient's initial compliance rate with drug prescriptions. By using this model, they categorized 69% of patients into a group that did not comply with the initial prescription. For example, the patient receives the prescription from the prescriber, and also drops it to a pharmacy, but never picks up the filled prescription from the pharmacy.

Barriers that affect the patient's compliance:

1. Cost of medications
2. Lack of access
3. Distance from the pharmacy
4. Transportation facilities
5. Psychological behavior of patients

Wellness and Health

Wellness is defined as an integrated method of functioning which is oriented towards maximizing the potential of which the individual is capable, within the environment where he or she is functioning.

Wellness normally involves the total person. The mind, body, and spirit are inseparable and constantly interact to determine one's experience and behavior.

It is seen as one's potential for wholeness and well-being, and is strongly influenced by personal choice and environmental factors.

3. Illness, Sickness and Disease

According to Eliot Freidson, illness is described as:

"One is immediately obligated to distinguish between illness as a purely biophysical state and illness as a human, social state. Illness as a biophysical state involves changes in bones, tissues, or vital fluids of any living organism. Illness as a social state involves changes in behavior that occur only among humans and that may vary with the culture."

A distinction between illness and disease:

Illness is defined by laymen as a reaction to perceived biological alteration while disease is defined by physicians, and for that reason, it is perceived to be a more precise term. The following sentences may help an individual to distinguish illness from a disease.

1. A person may have a disease and not be ill.
2. A person may be ill and not have a disease.
3. Both disease and illness may be present.

To understand more precisely, we can take the following example. Hypertension is a disease that has been defined by healthcare professionals as a combination of diastolic and systolic blood pressures outside "normal" limits. Now, it may be possible that a person with the disease of hypertension may be asymptomatic, and therefore not ill. And, as not being ill, this person may not seek care. An opposite of this can also be true. A person who experiences dizziness or headaches may perceive himself or herself as ill, seek care and be diagnosed as disease-free.

Practically, both these differences may have serious outcomes: failure to receive needed care in the first instance and a possible waste of medical resources in the second.

A definition of sickness:

Sickness is defined as a social state conferred on an individual by others. It is socially defined by sociologists.

According to Bezold, the state of health is determined by the interaction of the following variables:

1. Biology (e.g. generic determinants)
2. Behavior (e.g. smoking, drug abuse, eating habits)
3. Pre and post environments (including physical, biological, economical, and social)
4. The healthcare system

Types of Behaviors

There are three types of health-related behaviors:

1. Health Behavior
2. Illness Behavior
3. Sick Role Behavior

The pharmacist is most involved in the illness behavior, to a large extent in the sick role behavior, and in very few instances with the health behavior.

A. Health Behavior:

Any activity undertaken by a person who believes himself or herself to be healthy for the purpose of preventing disease or detecting disease in an asymptomatic stage.

Health behavior of people can be successfully expressed by the Health Belief Model. According to this model, people who step up to obtain preventive care or follow good nutrition and exercise in order to maintain good health are driven by the following factors:

1. The psychological effects of an individual (for example, a person whose father is suffering from diabetes will more likely be involved with preventive care than a person without such psychological effects.

2. The individual must also believe that a proposed action should be feasible and appropriate to use, and that it would reduce susceptibility to the condition or to the seriousness of the condition.

3. Some sort of cue or stimulus is needed to trigger an action response. For example, a person with poor eating habits may be convinced to pay more attention to eating habits if they are told they may cause ulcer or bowel problems in the long run.

Health Locus of Control Model and Health Behavior:

This is another theoretical model that is widely used to explain an individual health behavior. This model is usually administered to large population samples, and can be measured by a survey instrument.

Factors that affect individual health behavior under this model are:

1. Previous illness experience
2. Religious belief
3. Educational level
4. Economic status

The Fundamental Attribution Errors and Health (Survey Instrument):

An attribute is a characteristic or property that an individual has. For example, Steve is a handsome young man. The observer can assign another characteristic to him: I think he is an honest young man. In the above example, the observer is making an attribution based on what he noticed. However, an attribution made by an observer may be true or may not be. There are three possibilities:

1. Steve may always exhibit this trait (honesty).

   OR

2. Steve may exhibit this trait (honesty) only in certain situations.

   OR

3. Steve may seldom exhibit this trait (honesty).

In short, a potential difference exists between the observer's attribution and various situations that have not been observed by the observer. For example, in above case Steve may be a dishonest in most instances, however at the time when the observer is making an attribution, his behavior may likely give off an impression that he is an honest person.

Fundamental Attribution Error:

Normally, people tend to attribute traits to others, and to see their own behaviors in terms of the various situations in which they operate on a day to day basis. They see themselves as actors and interpret their responses as more of a response dependent on different situations while they observe others. Acting as observers, they tend to see stable characteristic in others (a stable characteristic does not vary by situations). Researchers have described this actor-observer tendency of people as "fundamental attribution error." It helps one to differentiate between acute symptoms (situations) and chronic symptoms (traits).

Take for example a pain related to headache. Many of us experience the headache on an infrequent basis and seek situational explanation for the cause of it. The headache may be because of poor sleep or due to a lack of coffee in the morning. In this example, we are responding to a symptom by seeking a situational explanation for the pain. For some people however, the symptoms of headache are more permanent. For example, a person who is suffering from migraine. For such a person, these symptoms become a characteristic of him. He is able to say he is healthy despite chronic disease (migraine headache) because he can do the things that he expects to be able to do.

Lewin's Three-Step Change Model:

Dissatisfaction with symptoms is the driving force behind a patient's action to visit a physician or a pharmacist. Symptoms that are unusual and associated with perceived risk, and that interfere with day to day function of the life, may often lead to action on the part of the patient. One way to summarize this change is with Lewin's unfreeze movement-refreeze change process.

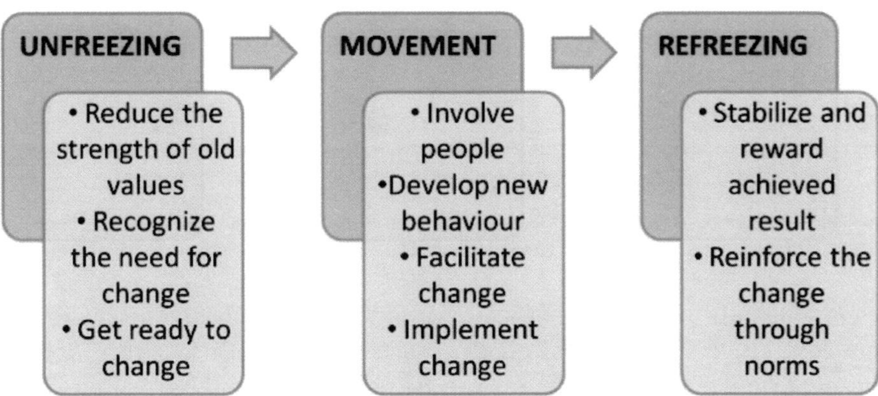

1. The process of change includes an initial phase where an individual must be "stuck" from existing ideas and behaviors. This is known as the "Unfreezing Phase." For example, Mr. Mehta has a habit of smoking. He smokes 10 to 15 cigarettes per day. This is called the **unfreezing phase**.

2. Once the individual is ready for change, he/she must be moved toward the desired behaviors, sometimes over a period of time. This phase is called "Movement." Due to heavy smoking, Mr. Mehta's lungs are not functioning properly, and a physician advised him to quit smoking. Mr. Mehta is now ready to quit smoking (change in behavior), and this phase is called **"Movement."**

3. However changing to new behaviors, is not enough. Those new activities must be solidified, habituated, and reinforced so that they continue over time. This phase is known as **"Refreezing"**. Referring to Mr. Mehta's case, six months after quitting smoking, he starts again. This is breaking off the phase "Refreezing." This phase requires a person to stick to a changed behavior.

Force Field Analysis:

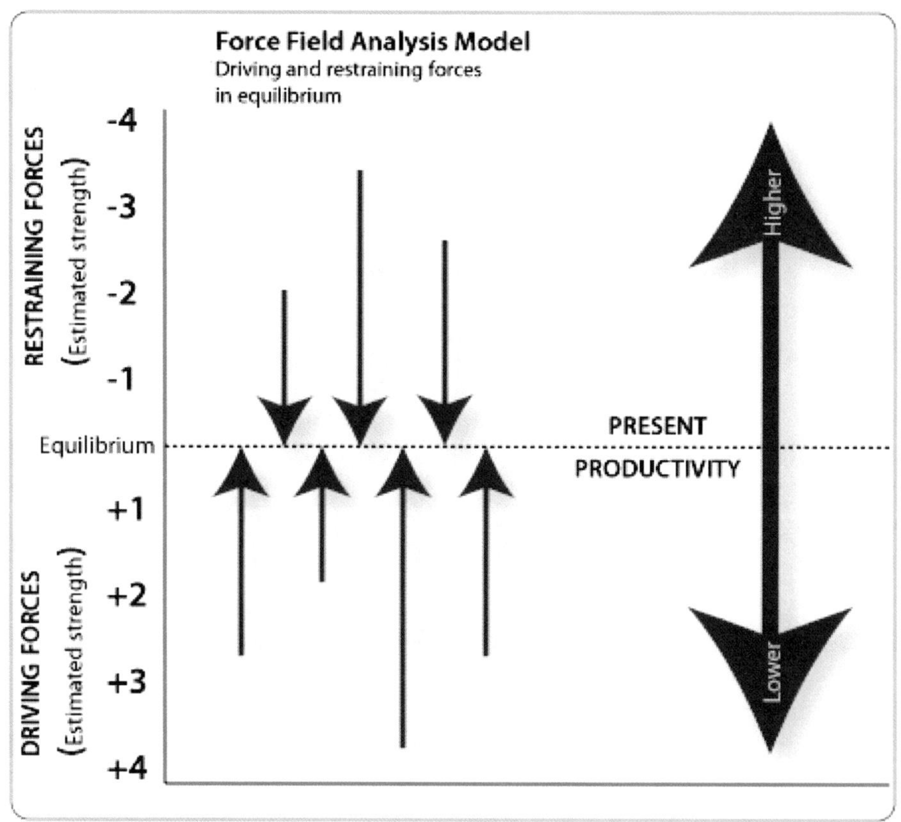

A Force Field Analysis is a useful tool for a healthcare provider in identifying the dynamic state in which the patient can be placed. In a routine life, forces change each day to both facilitate and inhibit the patient's response to the symptom of illness. A Force Field Analysis helps to visualize these various forces.

In above figure, there are two types of forces listed. Forces listed that encourage change are defined as driving forces, whereas the other forces that make change difficult are described as restraining forces. In a practical life, these forces are complex, and each may have dual characteristics of encouraging and preventing a change. Familiarizing with these forces may be helpful for patients as well as healthcare providers.

B. Illness Behavior:

Any activity undertaken by a person, who feels ill, for the purpose of defining the state of his health, and of discovering suitable remedy, is defined as **"Illness Behavior."** The "Sickness Career" helps with understanding the behavior of people when they are ill. The "Sickness Career" begins with a state of wellness. The changing from a state of wellness to illness is mainly depends on the presence and types of symptoms.

For example, many people-even those who feel well are able to identify some sort of symptoms at any given period of time. Often, they will view these symptoms as normal; however it is the intensity of the symptom that ultimately decides the change of one's status from being healthy to being sick.

According to Twaddle and Hessler, the following factors help determining the significant change in health status of an individual:

These factors are:

1. Interference with normal activities and functions (e.g. bowel habits, work ability)

2. Clarity of symptoms (sharp chest pain)

3. Tolerance threshold (some people can tolerate more pain, either because of personal characteristics, cultural factors, or the nature of their work)

4. Familiarity with symptoms (common symptoms that one has experienced previously, and recovered from are likely to be viewed as less serious than those that have not been previously experienced

5. Assumption about the cause (e.g. in the case of chest pain, it may be viewed as anything from heart attack to indigestion)

6. Assumption about prognosis (e.g. if long-term incapacity or possible death is associated with the symptom, it is likely to be viewed as more serious than the symptom without such intensity

7. Interpersonal influence

C. Sick Role Behavior:

Any activity undertaken by those who consider themselves ill for the purpose of getting well.

According to Talcott Parsons (Sociologist), the **Sick Role** consists of two rights and two duties.

Rights:
1. Freedom from blame for illness
2. Exemption from normal roles and tasks

These rights are appropriate only if a patient fulfills his/her duties.

Duties:
1. To do everything possible to recover
2. To seek technically competent help

The Sick Role gives an individual a reasonable excuse for making claims on others for care. People with symptoms (who are ill) can, with the confirmation (from a health care provider such as a physician), adopt the sick role (socially defined).

A person can enter the Sick Role if a physician confirms that the person is ill or if a family or friends of the person are willing to accept the status of "sick". Thus illness (individually defined) becomes sickness (socially defined), especially when the physician confirms the existence of a disease.

The following four factors play an important role in determining whether one is defined as "sick" or not.

1. **Legitimization by a physician:** A patient receives medical care from a physician. Prescriptions are important evidence of this factor.

2. **Symptoms:** A pain, discomfort or other manifestation that indicates change in health.

3. **Prognosis:** The expected outcome of the illness (e.g. probably will get worse, get better, stabilize, or is uncertain, etc.).

The Sick Role Behavior is a valuable tool in understanding the patient behavior; however this behavior does not apply to all cases. For example, using a Sick Role Behavior, how can one explain that a chronically ill patient will "recover"? In such instances, a patient (chronically ill) can adopt a Chronic Illness role.

Orthodox and Unorthodox Healing Systems

An orthodox healing system is defined as a healthcare related service that is scientifically and socially well accepted around the world (e.g. allopathic medicines and health-related services)

An unorthodox healing system is defined as a healthcare related service that is traditionally accepted but not socially (e.g. hydrotherapy, wave and radiation therapy, etc.).

Lists of normally employed unorthodox healing systems:

1. Physical therapy
2. Hydro therapy
3. Nutrition therapy
4. Plant-based therapy
5. Wave and radiation therapy
6. Mind and spirit healing
7. Self-exercise
8. Comprehensive system

1. **Physical therapy:** It can be further classified into the following categories:

a. Massage
b. Rolfing
c. Sensory awareness
d. Acupuncture
e. Reflexology

f. Moxibustion
g. Chiropractice

2. Hydrotherapy: It can be further classified into the following categories:

a. External hydrotherapy (e.g. baths and douches)
b. Internal hydrotherapy (e.g. colonic irrigation, enemas, inhalations)

3. Nutrition: It can be further classified into the following categories:

a. **Food supplement therapy**

Examples of food supplement therapies:

1. Apple cider vinegar
2. Molasses
3. Ginseng
4. Honey
5. Brewer's yeast

b. **Macrobiotics:** It is popularized in Japan. Foods are divided into yin or yang. By balancing yin and yang foods, one has an opportunity to achieve a balanced diet. Examples of such foods are:

	Yin food	Yang food
1.	Fruits and leaves	Dry food
2.	Hot aromatic food	Food growing below ground
3.	Food containing water	Salty or sour food
4.	Food grown in hot climates	Food grown in cold climates

4. Plant-based therapies: It can be further classified into the following categories:

a. Tincture
b. Aroma therapy
c. Herbal products

5. Wave and radiation based therapies: It can be further classified into the following categories:

a. Orgone therapy
b. Pyramid therapy

6. Mind and spirit healing therapies: It can be further classified into the following categories:

a. Biofeedback
b. Hypnosis
c. Spiritual healing
d. Meditation
e. Psychodrama

f. Primal therapies
g. Encounter groups
h. Sensitivity training
i. Translational analysis

7. Self-exercise:

a. Yoga
b. Sports
c. Dance
d. T'ai chi

8. Comprehensive system:

a. Ayurveda
b. Oriental medicine
c. Homeopathy

4. Prescribing Behavior of Healthcare Providers

It is very important to find out the prescribing behavior of practitioners since there is substantial evidence that prescription drugs are often used inappropriately. Prescribing errors are classified into two major categories:

1. Error of Commission: It includes those errors which are incorrectly written.

2. Error of Omission: It includes those errors in which the prescriber fails to specify a required element in the prescription (e.g. missing strength or dosage form). These errors can cause many problem for patients, ranging from decreased quality of life to unnecessary healthcare costs burden. Therefore, it is important to find out why practitioners prescribe in a certain fashion and how prescribing errors occur. To better understand prescribing errors and prescribing habits of practitioners, we can study a few models. These models will give us a better and clearer picture.

There are three different types of models that may help in studying the prescribing pattern of physicians:

1. Demographic and practice variables associated with prescribing
2. Psychosocial dynamics related to prescribing
3. Cognitive model of prescribing

1. Demographic and practice variables associated with prescribing:

Factors that affect prescribing decisions under demographic and practice variables model:

1. Physician's education
2. Physician's age
3. Physician's speciality
4. Physician's relationship with colleagues
5. Patient's gender
6. Patient's age
7. Patient's ethnicity

For example, the heart specialist-physician may have good knowledge about cardiac-related drugs, but less knowledge about psychiatric drugs when prescribing to a depressed patient.

2. Psychosocial dynamics related to prescribing model:

Psychosocial factors that affect physician's prescribing:

1. Prescription is a symbol of power and authority, and only practitioners have such power and authority to provide drugs.

2. Prescription is the way for physicians to express concern for patients.

3. Prescription is a powerful tool to end lengthy discussions and the patient's visit.

4. Prescription affirms that the patient is really ill.

3. Cognitive model of prescribing:

In this model, the prescribing decision of the prescriber merely depends on two major criteria:

1. The outcome of a prescribed drug.
2. The risk associated with a prescribed drug.

For example, if a patient is suffering from a mild illness, and a prescribed drug may cause serious and fatal reactions, it is unlikely that the prescriber will prescribe the drug to the patient. In contrast, if the patient is suffering from cancer or any other serious illness, it will force the prescriber to take the risk associated with the prescribed drug due to the seriousness of a disease.

In this model, the prescriber's concerns about drug attributes such as dosage, strength, duration and length of action of the prescribed drug, and correlates these attributes with drug's outcomes such as side or toxic effects of the drug, or cure rates of the drug. Thus, cognitive models of prescribing focus on which prescribing outcomes and drug attributes are really important when physicians make prescribing decisions.

The drug-choice model is a cognitive prescribing model related to Vroom's expectancy theory. Factors that affect the drug-choice model (selecting drugs for optimum benefit) are:

1. Control of disease by the prescribed drug
2. Patient's compliance with the prescribed drug
3. Side effects of the prescribed drug
4. Cost of the prescribed drug
5. Is the prescribed drug satisfying a patient's demand?
6. Criticism for colleagues

Sources of drug information that help physicians compare attributes and outcomes of drugs, and thus help in prescribing decisions.

1. Core education
2. Continuing education programs
3. Professional colleagues
4. Pharmaceutical advertising and pharmaceutical sales representatives
5. Patients may provide information about drugs through their previous clinical experience with drug therapy, or may request a specific drug be prescribed. Researchers believe that a patient's psychology is a major factor that affects the physician's prescribing decisions.

5. Theories of Human Inference

Theories of human inference can be used to evaluate and design educational methods that affect a physician's prescribing. The inference puts more emphasis on adverse or toxic reactions and effectiveness of drug therapy, since these two criteria are important factors that affect the physician's prescribing decisions. When prescribers make inference, they use one or more types of judgmental heuristics.

What is judgmental heuristics? **Heuristic** is defined as a rule of thumb, simplification, or educated guess that reduces or limits the search for solutions in domains that are difficult and poorly understood. Judgmental heuristics is defined as an educated guess which helps to classify and interpret new information, and drive us to make a final decision. We use these heuristics in our normal life constantly without realizing it. Most of the time they are accurate; however sometimes they may lead to judgmental errors. There are four types of judgmental heuristics that affect the prescriber's judgment. They are:

1. Representativeness heuristics
2. Availability heuristics
3. Framing heuristics
4. Anchoring heuristics

1. **Representativeness**: This type of heuristic involves a similarity between events or objects. For example, if a patient feels better after a drug is given, the prescriber may use judgment that the patient is cured, but the improvement could be a result of a number of other factors such as improved diet, normal fluctuation in the illness, decreased stress or using OTC therapies. Representativeness heuristic occurs when a physician does not consider these other factors in the outcome of therapy. This would not stop here; by using this judgment that the patient has been cured, the physician will prescribe the same drug in the future (from his previous experience) to other patients if he encounters similarity of symptoms of disease in patients.

2. **Availability heuristics**: This type of heuristic helps us judge frequency, probability and causality. According to this type of heuristic, new information is accessed according to information that is more readily available from memory. For example, a physician sees the same sort of symptom patterns frequently in a series of patients and makes an inference that a new patient with similar symptoms has the same illness. If proper clinical and laboratory tests are not used to verify the diagnosis, this could result in diagnosis error and inappropriate prescribing.

Availability heuristic is affected by vividness. Vivid pictures, stories and actual patient cases may be available more readily in memories and therefore affect the physician's judgment. It is easier to recall these images than statistics, graphs or figures when making a diagnosis. Prescribing can be affected by these images through vividness.

3. **Framing heuristics:** This type of judgmental heuristic occurs when physicians use another alternative to avoid an undesirable outcome. For example, a particular drug may cause cancer when used for a prolonged time for 1 in 1000,000 patients. A prescribing physician may put more emphasis on undesirable outcomes when making a prescribing decision, even though the drug has the best clinical effects for the given diagnosis. The best example of framing is saccharine (sweetener) which was taken off the market due to association with cancer in rats when given in large doses.

4. **Anchoring heuristics**: Another type of heuristic is anchoring. Most of us make initial assessments and decisions until we find correct answers. However, sometimes our adjustments are not adequate to support our initial assessment since we are under high influence of the initial assessment. This resistance to change from initial decision is called anchoring. For example, a practitioner makes an initial assessment (from experience and sets of symptoms) and prescribes a drug to a patient until he receives results from laboratory or diagnostic tests. The anchoring occurs when the prescriber fails to discontinue the drug even after laboratory or diagnostic tests indicate that it is not needed.

6. Barriers To Interprofessional Relations

There are a number of barriers that prevent an effective communication between pharmacists and other healthcare professionals. Out of these, attitude, time, and knowledge are major concerns.

1. Attitude
2. Time and money
3. Skill and knowledge

1. Attitude: The attitude is the most common barrier that prevents the effective communication between pharmacists and prescribers. The attitudes and expectations of pharmacists are developed on the basis of previous experience. Due to complex health care settings, pharmacists believe that physicians are usually unapproachable, and therefore many pharmacists simply avoid contacting the physician unless it is strictly necessary. One of the conferences in the UK reported that "pharmacists see doctors as diagnosticians' whereas physicians see themselves as a last resource to provide health- related services to patients, and physicians see pharmacists as medication dispensers, while pharmacists see themselves as drug experts."

2. Time and money: The lack of time is an excuse provided by pharmacists to avoid communication with other healthcare professionals. However, it is also true that many pharmacists work in retail setting have no sufficient help to provide extended health related services to patients. It is plan administrator responsibility to provide adequate help and financial incentive to pharmacists to encourage them to extend their services beyond dispensing. This way, a healthcare cost can be effectively controlled (e.g. by preventing drug interactions or eliminating a duplicate therapy before dispensing) and optimum therapeutic outcomes can be achieved.

3. Skill and knowledge: The lack of skill and knowledge may prevent many pharmacists from offering counseling to patients. This may happen when pharmacists are not in touch with their colleagues or avoid communication with other healthcare professionals. A major barrier is the inability of pharmacists to communicate with physicians due to the anticipation of attitudes from prescribers. Also, pharmacists may not have all the information about a patient's current medication history, which may lead to poor communication with patients.

How To Improve Interprofessional Relationships

Effective communication skills play an important role in building up successful interprofessional relationships with prescribers or patients.

Many pharmacy courses now put more emphasis on effective communication skills i.e. the skills of maintaining ongoing relationships, empathy, body language when interviewing or doing patient counseling, and effectively providing information to ensure optimum benefits.

According to Quintrell, a professional and confident approach must be implemented in order to provide successful and effective communication. He states: "As a pharmacist, you have the right to your professional existence and your professional opinion, and the right to have that existence and opinion respected."

Most interprofessional relationships are based on mutual respect. How can a pharmacist expect a professional interchange from a prescriber when he is criticizing the physician's prescribing habits?

According to Quintrell, there are four important stages in the process of interchange. They are:

1. Statement
2. Reply
3. Negotiation
4. Resolution

1. **Statement**: This stage consists of a clear and confident statement about the situation without apologies or indecisions.

2. **Reply**: In this stage a person (pharmacist) has to carefully and respectfully listen to the needs and wishes of the other person (prescriber).

3. **Negotiation**: In this stage, a person (pharmacist) may offer help to the other person (physician) with reasonable negotiation.

4. **Resolution**: This is the final stage in which both parties have to focus on problem resolutions, primarily keeping the patient's benefits in mind.

7. Consumer Behavior Models

Consumer Behavior Models help us to understand what factors drive the consumer to make a purchase decision, whether the goods are groceries or an expensive car. There are mainly two types of consumer behavior models. They are:

1. Howard Buyer Behavior Model
2. EKB Buyer Behavior Model

1. **Howard Buyer Behavior Model**: This was first proposed by John Howard and Jagdish Sheth in their book The Theory of Buyer Behavior. According to the Howard Model, factors that affect the purchase decisions of buyers are:

1. Purchase intention
2. Brand attitude
3. Brand comprehension

Brand attitude relies on information related to products exposed to the consumer's, consumer previous experience with the company's product, and consumer judgment about the new product or service of interest.

2. **EKB Buyer Behavior Model:** This model was first proposed by Engel-Kollat-Blackwell researchers at Columbia University. The key elements that drive consumers to purchase goods or services under this model are:

1. Recognition of a problem
2. Information search
3. Alternative evaluation
4. Product choice
5. Outcomes

The first element that the consumer thinks about is identifying the problem. For example, if Russel's car gives him trouble for 2 to 3 days, this will drive him to think about whether to fix the car or buy a new car. The second step is to search for information related to the problem. In the above case, Russel tries to find information from various sources (newspaper, television or internet) to purchase a new car. After the search is completed, an alternative evaluation about the product or service has been conducted.

For example, which model or type of car should be selected? The next step is to finalize the product from the available alternatives. The final step will be the outcome of a purchase decision. For example, are you satisfied with the car you purchased? Depending on the outcome, future buying decisions will be made.

Purchase Decisions and Types of Involvement

There are two types of involvement associated with purchase decisions. One is called high involvement purchase decision and the other is low involvement purchase decision. High involvement purchase decisions are risky, time-consuming and long-term (For example, buying a house, a car or home appliances). Most consumers are not aware of the risk associated with high involvement purchases; moreover these types of products or services are not easily exchangeable if they are not satisfied with them.

In contrast, the low involvement purchases are easy to make, less time-consuming and short-term (For example, buying a groceries, toothbrush or toothpaste etc).

On the basis of the above concepts, Everette conducted a random search to find out which factors affect patient's buying decisions for expensive medications. According to him, the following elements play an important role in encouraging or discouraging patients from purchasing prescription drugs. These elements are:

1. Side effects of a prescribed drug (97%)
2. Physician's recommendation (90%)
3. Strength of prescribed medication (73%)
4. Prior use and experiences with prescribed medications (72%)
5. Price of prescribed medicines (58%)
6. The availability of generic versions (51%)

Model of Consumer Choice in Medication Use

The important elements of this model are that it helps in the decision-making and problem solving behaviors of consumers.

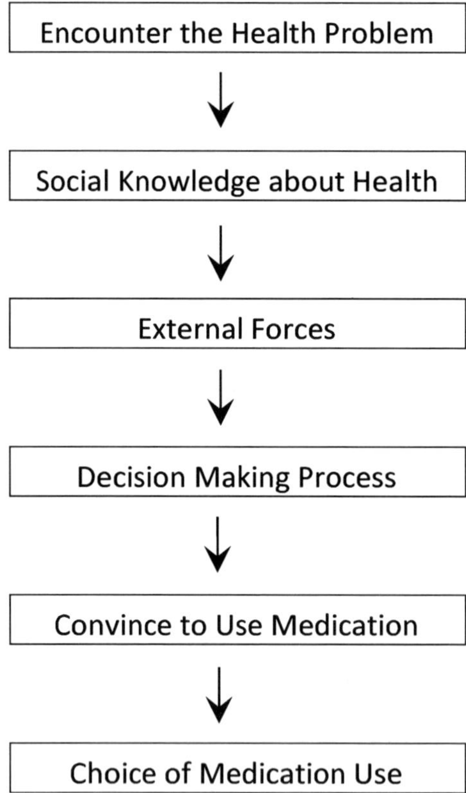

According to this model, consumer medication behaviors usually begin when the person encounters a health problem or anticipates that he or she is at risk of getting sick.

Once a person sees himself as sick, he starts looking for a remedy. For this purpose, he seeks help from social factors (social knowledge of health and illness) and external forces such as media, promotional advertising, or face to face interaction with other people.

Finally, a decision-making process begins. Under this process, consumer choice and use of medication is affected by a number of other elements such as behavioral, social and cultural factors.

Out of these, social network plays an important role in the consumer's choice of medications. Social networks are those sets of contacts or relationships with others through which individuals maintain a social identity and receive ideas, information, services, social support, and the opportunity to develop new social contacts. These social networks are also known as lay referral networks and mainly consist of relatives and friends the consumer normally consults for guidance.

Below is the list of social and behavioral factors that affect consumer choice for medication. These are:

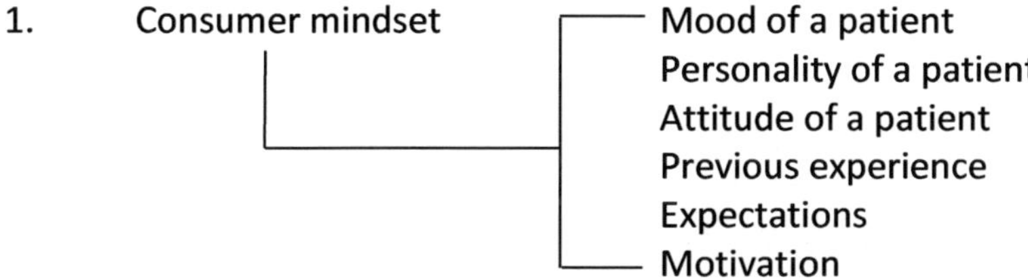

2. Knowledge about symptoms
3. Drugs-related information
4. Drugs' availability
5. Advertisement through media
6. Lay referral network
7. Healthcare professional advice
8. Accessibility of drugs

8. Different Models of Patient-Practitioner Relationship

There are three different models that describe patient-practitioner relationship. They are:

1. Paternalistic model or expert model
2. Social conflict model
3. Engineering model

1. **Paternalistic model or expert model:** It is the oldest model. This model assumes that healthcare providers will make all major decisions for the patient, and the patient has to rely and obey the decision of the practitioner. Proponents of this model can often be detected by phrases such as "speaking as your physician, I believe you should...."

2. **Social contract model:** This model believes and focuses on the need for genuine human interaction in the patient-practitioner relationship. This model assumes the mutual participation (from patients and prescribers) in the decision making process.

3. **Engineering model:** Under this model, a prescriber takes no responsibility for the final health-related decisions of his patients. Health professionals who adopt this model view themselves as scientists, and believe they deal only with facts. The health professional goal under this model is to present all the facts to their patients so that patients make their own decisions about the best course of action to take.

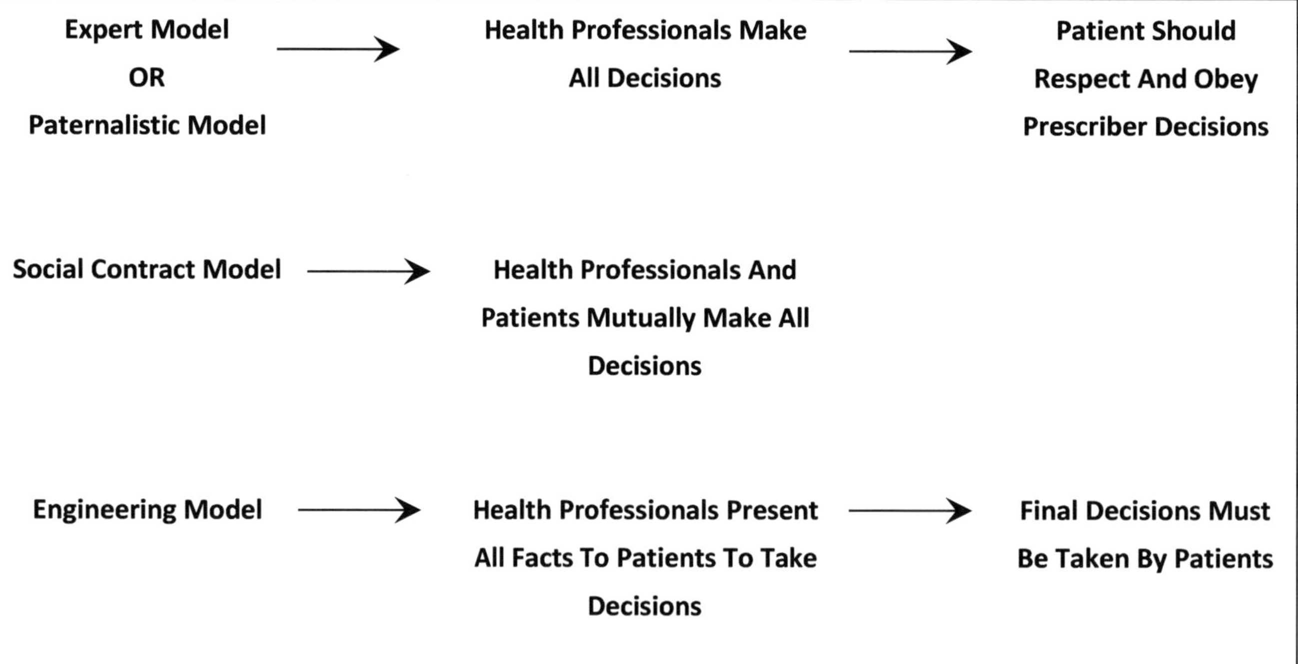

Szasz-Hollender Model of Doctor-Patient Relationships

Three other models were presented by Thomas Szasz and Mark Hollender. They are:

1. Activity-Passivity Model
2. Guidance Corporation Model
3. Mutual Participation Model

1. **Activity-Passivity Model:** The social prototype of this model is one of parent to infant. The health professional role is somewhat like the parent in this model and the patient represents the infant.

The physicians take charge and make decisions to provide optimum care to patients. Treatment takes place regardless of the patient's wishes. In most cases, the patient is not aware of what is happening to him or her, and is unable to participate in the decision making process.

For example, a patient has an acute life threatening trauma, severe bleeding, diabetic coma or heart strokes.

2. **Guidance-Corporation Model:** This model represents the relationship of a parent to an older child or an adolescent.

The physician guides a patient as to what to do, and the patient is expected to cooperate and comply with the physician's advice and decision.

In this model, a patient is aware of what is going on and is capable of making and analyzing decisions. This model works best for patients with acute infections, broken bones, or early stages of diagnostic chronic disease.

3. **Mutual Participation:** It is the prototype of the social contract model.

The physician's and patient's role is somewhat similar to adult-adult interaction.

Under this type of model, a patient takes the full responsibility of his or her own welfare. Patients suffering from chronic illnesses such as diabetes, arthritis, or hypertension and patients with psychological problems, fall under this model.

9. A Model for Analyzing The Medication Use Process

This model was first proposed by Anderson and Newman. This model consists of three stages. These are:

1. Predisposing factors
2. Enabling factors
3. Need for care variables

1. **Predisposing factors:** These factors are those which make a patient think to buy a medication. For example, Third-Party insurance coverage may affect the patient's thinking about buying or purchasing a particular product.

A list of predisposing factors:

1. Doctor
2. Pharmacist
3. Age of a patient
4. Sex of a patient
5. Media exposure
6. Marital status of a patient
7. Family background of a patient
8. Cost of medication
9. Third-Party coverage

2. **Enabling factors:** It is the next step to buy a particular drug or product once the predisposing phase is over.

A list of enabling factors:

1. Doctor
2. Pharmacist
3. Family background of a patient
4. Education of a patient
5. Severity of symptoms
6. Income status of a patient
7. Third-Party coverage

3. **Need for care variable:** This is an important factor to understand the medication use process of patients. According to Verbrugge, sick people would use medications and people who are sick would not. This statement is supported by the fact that every sickness cannot be easy to diagnose.

10. Noncompliance and Factors Affecting Noncompliance

What is noncompliance and why is it so important?

In a simple term, noncompliance means a patient's resistance to treating his underlying disease. This could range from not filling prescribed medications to avoiding visiting a physician's office at all. It is important to identify noncompliance and treat it correctly. For example, a patient spends time and money to see a physician, obtain a diagnosis and a prescription, and then either not have the prescription filled at all (initial compliance) or not taking the medication properly.

Noncompliance costs the healthcare industry more than $500 billion annually. For example, a patient is suffering from hypertension and may not regularly take his medicine, and end up in the emergency room. Thus by not comply with the prescribed therapy, a patient may increase the cost and burden on the healthcare industry.

There are four forms of compliances. These are:

1. Initial compliance
2. Partial compliance
3. Compliance
4. Hyper compliance

1. **Initial compliance**: This occurs when a patient receives a prescription from a prescriber, and transfers it to a pharmacy, but never picks up the filled prescription from the pharmacy.

2. **Partial compliance**: The process of taking a prescribed and dispensed medication at a level less than the prescriber or dispenser intended.

3. **Compliance**: The process in which a patient sticks to and follows a prescribed and dispensed regimen closely, as the prescriber or dispenser intended. Compliance may also be referred as therapeutic end point (e.g. by taking a diabetic pill regularly {compliance}, a therapeutic end point can be achieved {normal blood glucose level}).

4. **Hyper compliance:** The process in which a patient takes a prescribed and dispensed regimen at a level over or above the recommended and intended dosing intervals prescribed and dispensed by healthcare professionals.

Detection of Noncompliance

Self-reports and interviews with patients are the most common and simplest methods for determining compliance with therapy. Noncompliance can be detected two ways:

1. Indirect methods
2. Direct methods

1. **Indirect Assessment for Detecting Compliance:**

a. Patients' self-reports
b. Therapeutic outcomes

c. Physician estimates (avoiding physician's visit)
d. Pharmacist estimates (medications not refilled and not picked up by a patient)
e. Family interviews

2. Direct Assessment for Detecting Noncompliance:

1. Blood serum assays
2. Urine assays

Noncompliance rates for specific conditions:

	Conditions	Noncompliance rates
1.	Arthritis	55 to 71%
2.	Diabetes	40 to 50%
3.	Hypertension	40%
4.	Epilepsy	30 to 50%
5.	Asthma	20%
6.	Contraception	8%

The most commonly stated reasons for noncompliance:

	Statements	% of Total
1.	Forgetfulness	39.6%
2.	Side effects	17.7%
3.	Drug perceived as not necessary	12.5%
4.	Confusion	11.5%
5.	Cost	10.4%

Factors Affecting Noncompliance

1. Patient's age: Elderly people have a lower compliance rate compared to young people.
2. Patient's sex: Women have a higher compliance rate compared to men.
3. Patient's education level: An educated patient seems to be more complied compare to an uneducated patient.
4. Patient's family background.
5. Dosage form of a drug: A pill or an oral solution has a higher compliance rate compared to a parenteral dosage form.
6. A number of drugs: As a number of drugs in regimen increases, the compliance rate decreases.
7. Medication regimen: A once daily drug regimen has a higher compliance rate than an every 4 to 6 hours drug-regimen.
8. Type of illness
9. Patient-prescriber relationship
10. Patient's nature: The perceived importance of the drug is more important than the drug itself.

11. Prescription Errors and Pharmacists' Responsibility

Error: According to an IOM report, an error is defined as the failure of a planned action to be completed as intended (e.g. error of execution) or the use of a wrong plan to achieve an aim (e.g. error of planning). Thus an error may result from actions that do not go as intended, for example correctly reading a prescription but dispensing the wrong dose of the drug; or where the intended action is the wrong one, for example making an incorrect recommendation.

According to Abood, dispensing errors are classified in two different categories:

1. **Mechanical dispensing error:** It is an error that may occur in the preparation or processing of the prescription.

2. **Judgmental dispensing error:** It is an error of discretion in counseling, screening, or patient drug monitoring.

An analysis of malpractice claims suggests that mechanical errors account for 86% of liability claims. The majority of claims are associated with the wrong drug being dispensed.

A workload issue is the primary cause for making the error. It has been found that 60% of pharmacists dispensing more than 100 prescriptions per day reported having made an error.

The greatest risk (for error) was felt by pharmacists working in mail order pharmacies, traditional chains, and hospital pharmacies, followed by individual community base pharmacists.

The prescription volume is cited as the most significant factor in the dispensing errors. In one survey, most pharmacists agreed it was safe to dispense 17 prescriptions per hour or 150 prescriptions in a 9-hour shift.

Abood has also proposed a list of "stress reducers" that might reduce pharmacist error. The list of suggestions includes:

1. A pharmacy must provide a comfortable waiting area for patients in order to reduce "patient pressure" on pharmacists.

2. A pharmacy must encourage the use of electronic devices such as faxes and voice mail in order to minimize the number of interruptions and distractions.

3. A pharmacy must encourage the physician to use electronic prescribing in order to reduce handwritten errors.

4. A pharmacist must also adopt the habit of counseling. This will give him a break from routine dispensing. Abood also added that pharmacists must use the "show and tell" technique during counseling, where the pharmacist shows the medication to the patient while asking the patient pertinent questions, such as how the physician advises you to take medications or for what purpose he prescribed these medicines to you? These maneuvers will help pharmacist's to detect an error before the patient leaves the pharmacy.

The National Coordinating Council for Medication Error Reporting and Prevention (NCCMERP) defines a medication error as "any preventable event that may cause or lead to inappropriate medication use or patient harm while the medication is in the control of the health care professional, patient, or consumer".

Types of medication errors:

1. **Prescribing:** The inappropriate selection of a drug or drug therapy by the prescriber, or incorrect or inadequate instructions for use.

2. **Transcription:** The failure to transcribe information or the improper entry of an order into an information system.

3. **Dispensing:** The failure to dispense medication as prescribed, or to provide appropriate labeling.

4. **Administration:** A discrepancy between the drug therapy received and the drug therapy intended.

5. **Monitoring:** The failure to review a prescribed regimen for appropriate treatment or to assess patient response to therapy.

6. **Patient Adherence:** Failure by a patient to take medication(s) as prescribed.

Factors that may cause or contribute to medication errors:

1. Unavailable drug information (such as lack of up-to-date warnings).

2. Miscommunication of drug orders, which can involve poor handwriting, confusion between drug with similar names, misuse of zeroes and decimal points, confusion of metric and other dosing units, and inappropriate abbreviations.

3. Lack of appropriate labeling when a drug is prepared and repackaged into smaller units.

4. Environmental factors such as lighting, heat, noise, and interruptions that can distract health care professionals from their medical tasks

5. Complex or poorly designed technology.

6. Poor procedures or techniques.

7. Job stress and dose miscalculations.

8. Deficiencies related to knowledge of drug therapy.

9. General failure to act in accordance with education and training.

10. Incorrect diagnosis.

11. Patient misuse of medication due to lack of patient information or education.

Strategies to avoid medication errors:

1. Verify if patients have any allergies and/or reactions to medications.

2. Inquire of patients if they have any current medical conditions, particularly diabetes, kidney disease, liver disease, cardiovascular disease, and psychiatric disease.

3. Ask patients about medications they are currently taking, including any nonprescription products, vitamins and minerals, and herbals.

4. Try to standardize use of height and weight measurements, preferably using metric units.

5. Make sure drug information databases are up to date.

6. Compile a list of high-alert medications, ie, medications that require extra precautions when administered, prescribed, dispensed, or refilled.

7. Compile a list of similar drug names and circulate it among pharmacy staff, and do not store these drugs near each other.

8. Ensure patients are aware of the indication for which a drug is prescribed.

Patients and pharmacists need to work together to reduce the occurrence of medication errors. The key is enhanced communication; in which pharmacists inform patients about the medications they are prescribed. Listed below are some examples of information pharmacists should provide.

1. The name of the drug and its indications
2. Correct dosing, including time to take it and whether or not to take with food
3. Common side effects
4. Possible drug-drug interactions, including with OTCs
5. Possible food-drug interactions
6. To have patients check the medication label prior to leaving the pharmacy to ensure they are receiving the correct medication

Due to increased incidences of dispensing errors by pharmacists, many states and the federal government have proposed institutional programs and regulations to address the impact of errors.

For example, Florida state has emphasized an educational approach. Under this new regulation, no new pharmacist will be granted a license and no license will be renewed unless an approved 2-hour course on medication errors has been completed.

Many states are also trying to establish error-reporting systems. Connecticut state is the perfect example in this matter. According to new Connecticut pharmacy law, each pharmacy must post a sign in a conspicuous location, and also include a statement on the bag containing the prescription that: "If you have a concern that an error may have occurred in the dispensing of your prescription, you may contact the Department of Consumer Protection Drug Control Division." A phone number to contact the institution must be provided.

In 2001, Maryland state passed a patient safety act. Under this new act, a pharmacist has to follow certain new regulations in order to minimize dispensing errors. These new regulations are:

1. Pharmacists must establish methods to educate patients in preventing medication errors.

2. Pharmacists must ensure that all staffs receive an annual education in preventing errors, and defining "high-alert" medications.

3. In addition to these rules, the state is also expected to develop rules requiring hospitals to report all medical errors resulting in serious harm.

In June 2002, California passed new state regulations requiring each pharmacy to establish a quality assurance program prevent to medication errors. A medication error is defined as any variation in the prescription order that may harm a patient. The quality assurance program documents and assesses all medication errors to determine their course and an appropriate response. This is to be used to develop pharmacy systems and processes to prevent future errors. An investigation of the error by the pharmacy is to commence no later than two business days after the error is discovered.

The Washington State Department of Health passed an interesting proposal that the legislature should ban handwritten prescriptions by 2005.

North Carolina State Board of Pharmacy believes that work load issue is major root cause of dispensing errors. The Board has advised all management staff of pharmacies to reexamine their policy as workload increase. Through a new regulation, the board set 150 prescriptions per pharmacist per day as the limit for safe dispensing.

Adverse Drug Events

Adverse Drug Event (ADE): An adverse drug event (ADE) can be defined as any injury resulting from the use of a drug. ADEs can be further classified as follows:

1. **Medication Error:** Any preventable drug event that may cause or lead to inappropriate medication use or harm to a patient.

2. **Adverse Drug Reaction (ADR):** Any response to a drug that is noxious and unintended and that occurs at doses normally used in humans for the prophylaxis, diagnosis, or therapy of disease.

3. **Therapeutic Failure:** A suboptimal response to the drug therapy.

4. **Adverse Drug Withdrawal Event:** A noxious or unintended response that occurs when a drug is discontinued.

5. **Accidental/Intentional Overdose:** An adverse drug event due to a super therapeutic level of a drug, either accidental (child poisoning) or intentional (suicide attempt).

Quality and Improving Quality of Care

What is Quality?

According to Merriam Webster's College Dictionary, quality is defined as "degree of excellence" or "superiority in kind." This concept of quality is not only limited to healthcare. As consumers we always look for quality products, whether it is selecting a restaurant for dinner, buying clothes or reserving airline tickets for travelling. We always gather the information available for a particular product and justify its price with the quality of the product.

Components of Quality in health care setting

1. Appropriateness of Therapy (i.e. the right care is provided at the right time)
2. Technical Excellence (i.e. care is provided in the correct manner)
3. Accessibility of Care (i.e. care can be obtained when needed)
4. Acceptability of Care (i.e. patients are satisfied with provided care)

Quality of Care vs. Quantity of Care

There are many times quality of care is confused with quantity of care. More care does not necessarily equal better care. However, when rating for quality of care, unintentionally we always look for quantity of service (i.e. how many services are received.)

The relationship between quantity and quality of care is complex and also unique. For example, there are times when the quality of care is rated poor because of quantitative inadequacy.

The perfect example of this would be the failure to complete the vaccination series. In order to receive successful therapeutic outcomes, and therefore a good quality of care, one must complete the whole set of vaccinations. Thus in this case quantitative inadequacy may lead to poor quality of care.

In contrast, care can be excessive and even harmful. Such care is not only costly but of equal or lower quality. For example, the care associated with annual pap smears and routine use of fetal sonograms in patients with a low risk of pregnancies. These types of cares are unnecessary, and may increase overall expenditure of healthcare. Although, they are used excessively but carry very little risk.

Other care such as routine chest x-ray examinations and annual dental x-rays are not only used excessively, but they are associated with potential dangers due to exposed x-radiations. These types of care are used unnecessarily, and not only that, they are extensively harmful to patients. Such care must be avoided, and used only when they are really required. This way the quality of care can be improved and cost of healthcare can be controlled.

In addition to unnecessary and excessive care, there is inefficient care. In such cases, reducing the costs of care can be achieved by producing it more efficiently; not by reducing the quantity or intensity of care but by substituting with another alternative.

Substitution of a nurse practitioner for a physician or the use of ambulatory rather than inpatient surgery are two examples where good quality can be maintained while reducing costs.

How To Measure The Quality?

The quality of healthcare can be measured by approaching and gathering information about its structure, process, and outcome.

1. **Structure:** According to Donabedian, a structure has been defined as "the relatively stable characteristics of the providers of care, of the tools and resources they have at their disposal, and of the physical and organization settings in which they work."

   Examples of structures are board certification of physicians, nurse/bed ratios for hospitals, availability and accessibility of facilities, availability of laboratory services for HMOs, etc.

   Structure is an indirect measure of quality. It is useful to the degree that it can influence the direct provision of care.

2. **Process:** It concerns the set of activities that go on between physicians and patients. Process is what is done to patients.

3. **Outcomes:** It is defined as a result of an implemented activity. In this case, it would be the therapeutic result of an intervention. It normally helps to find out how an implemented therapy works on patients.

The Causal Model For Quality

The causal model helps assessing the quality. Normally, a structure influences the process of care, which in turn affects the outcome of care. It has been stated by many sociologists that the application of the appropriate process of care can maximize the therapeutic outcome of the care.

The most important thing is the link between structure, process and outcome. Many research methods have been developed to identify and justify these links. For example, are board certified physicians (structure) more likely to make appropriate use of laboratory tests (process)? And does the appropriate utilization of the laboratory tests have a positive effect on patient recovery (outcomes)? Structural indicators (e.g. nurse/bed ratios) are easy and inexpensive to access, whereas information on process (e.g. prescribing patterns of physicians for laboratory tests) and outcome of care (the effect of appropriate utilization of laboratory tests on patient health) are expensive, and often unavailable to obtain.

The Casual Model will help us to identify alternative treatments with fewer side effects and the same therapeutic outcomes of an intervention (therefore more quality care). For example, in one study, family physicians were found to be less likely than obstetricians to use epidural anesthesia, cesarean sections, and other interventions with low risk deliveries, and these differences in the process of care did not affect clinical outcomes of care (safe deliveries). Thus family physicians (structure) without use of epidural anesthesia (process) may provide the same therapeutic outcome (safe delivery) and thus, this shows the better quality of care compared to obstetricians (another structure).

Principles of Pharmacoeconomics

12. ECHO Model and Economic Outcomes

ECHO Model: It is also known as the Economic, Clinic, and Humanistic Outcomes Model. This model normally relates to a disease and therapeutic outcomes (related to disease) to assist physicians in the decision-making process.

Economic Evaluation: It is a process by which costs and consequences related to health-care industry can be assessed. The most important step in conducting an economic evaluation is to find the prospective from which the study was conducted and the audience for which it was intended. For example, an economic analysis of two antihypertensive medications provides the same level of therapeutic benefit.

However, drug A is significantly less costly than drug B. Another important difference between these two drugs is their side effects profiles. Drug A has a major side effect of causing arrhythmia, whereas drug B is devoid of such adverse effects.

From the perspective of third party companies, drug A may be the better choice due to low cost, however from the patient's perspective-whose out of pocket costs are minimal-drug B would be a better choice due to the low side effects profile. Therefore, it is really important to find out the perspective from which the result will be viewed.

Costs and Consequences Associated with Economic Analysis

Cost associated with economic analysis is divided into four major groups:

1. Direct Cost
2. Direct Nonmedical Cost
3. Indirect Cost
4. Intangible Cost

1. **Direct Cost:** These are expenses directly associated with medical care due to illness. Examples of such costs are:

a. Medication related costs
b. Physician's visit expenses
c. Hospitalization costs
d. Laboratory and diagnostic test expenses
e. Adverse drug reaction treatment costs
f. Specialist consultation cost

2. **Direct Nonmedical Costs:** They are primarily related to out-of-pocket expenses incurred by patients during illness. Examples of such costs are:

a. Transportation costs to hospitals or clinics
b. Accommodation costs for family during major illness
c. Costs related to meals and dining during hospitalization

Cost	Examples
Direct Medical Cost	Drug Hospitalization Laboratory Tests
Direct Non-Medical Cost	Transportation
Indirect Costs	Reduced Productivity Days Lost From Work
Intangible Costs	Pain Suffering

Outcomes	Examples
Economic Outcomes	Cost
Clinical Outcomes	Blood Pressure Blood Glucose Mortality Number of Reoccurrences Number of Disease Free Patients
Humanistic Outcomes	Quality of Life Patient Satisfaction Patient Preferences

Method-Type	Cost Measure	Outcome Measure
Cost of Illness	$	N/A
Cost Minimization Analyses	$	Any (generally clinical) e.g. Blood pressure monitoring

Cost Effective Analyses	$	Clinical (Physical Unit)
Cost Utility Analyses	$	Quality Adjusted Life Years Gained (QALY)
Cost Benefit Analyses	$	$

---

3. **Indirect Costs:** These costs are associated with morbidities and mortalities due to illness. Examples of such costs are:

a. Loss of work due to illness
b. Lost earning due to permanent death

4. **Intangible Costs:** These types of costs are a result of psychological factors such as pain, side effects of treatments, stress, or depression due to illness. Examples of such costs are:

1. Quality of life
2. Psychological factors

Consequences/Benefits

Similar to costs, benefits or consequences can be subdivided into three major categories:

1. Direct Benefits
2. Indirect Benefits
3. Intangible Benefits

1. **Direct Benefits:** These would include prevention of future illness and thereby a reduction of health-related expenses, a reduction of insurance premiums, and a reduction of healthcare-related services (e.g. hospitalization, physician's visit).

2. **Indirect Benefits:** These would include an avoidance of physical disability or death.

3. **Intangible Benefits:** These would include an absence of pain and improved quality of life.

Cost/Benefit Valuation

A. **Assigning Costs:** The next step is to assign a dollar value to all costs and benefits that are identified during an economic evaluation study. To assign a dollar value to direct costs is simple and straightforward, but assigning a dollar value to indirect costs and benefits is even more complex.

There are two important methods which help assigning a dollar value to indirect costs and benefits. These are:

1. The Human Capitol Approach Method
2. The Willingness-To-Pay Method

1. **The Human Capitol Approach Method:** In this method, the value of human work and life is calculated by the economic productivity of the individual. This method allows us to calculate and correlate actual market income of an individual or groups of individuals with lost resources and profit related to illness. For example, under this study, if an average annual income of a pharmacist is set at $70,000, then the cost or expenses related to missing work due to illness can be calculated.

   The only disadvantage associated with this method is that when equating or assigning the market income for the particular profession, the market price does not reflect the true value of an individual. For example, what if an individual is a pharmacist manager making over $120,000. Another disadvantage of this method is that it does not consider children, elderly, or full-time homemakers while conducting the study.

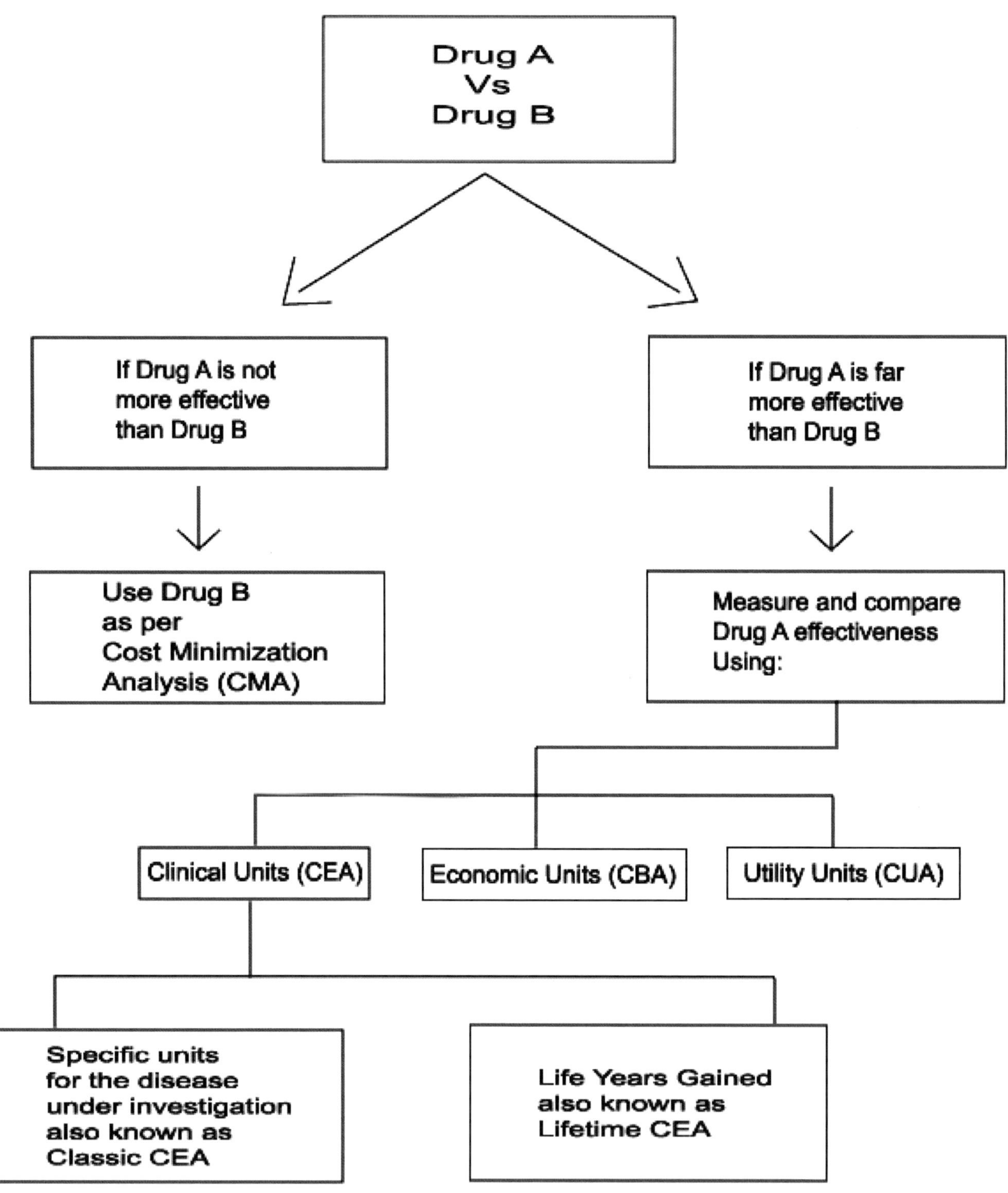
Drug A
Vs
Drug B
If Drug A is not
more effective
than Drug B
If Drug A is far
more effective
than Drug B
Use Drug B
as per
Cost Minimization
Analysis (CMA)
Measure and compare
Drug A effectiveness
Using:
Clinical Units (CEA)
Economic Units (CBA)
Utility Units (CUA)
Specific units
for the disease
under investigation
also known as
Classic CEA
Life Years Gained
also known as
Lifetime CEA

2. **The Willingness-To-Pay Method:** This method assigns a value to benefits and indirect costs by determining what the individual is willing to pay for preventing negative or receiving positive effects of an intervention. The disadvantage associated with this method is that there is always conflict between the price people are willing to pay and the price they are actually able to pay.

B. **Discounting:** When assigning a dollar value to costs or benefits, one must consider the effect of time on such costs or benefits. The future costs and benefits should be valued lower than the present costs and benefits since a dollar invested today is worth more than a dollar invested in the future. Therefore, it is essential to discount the future costs or benefits before being incorporated into the economic analysis.

There is another question that arises during analysis: Which type of health-related outcomes or costs should be discounted, and what discount rate should be used? Most economists select the discount range from 3 to 6%. By using the following equation, one can calculate the discounted values.

$PV = FC \times (1 + DR)^{-n}$ where,

PV = present value
FC = future cost
DR = discount rate
n = the number of years cost will be incurred in the future

For example, if we want to implement a new program that will take a period of 4 years with a cost of $10000 per year. By using a discount rate of 6% (0.06), the present value of the plan would be:

$PV = 10{,}000 \times (1 + .06)^{-1}$
PV = $ 9433 (for the first year)

$PV = 10{,}000 \times (1 + .06)^{-2}$
PV = $ 8890 (for the second year)

Thus, with a discount rate of 6%, the cost incurred would be $34650 ($9430 + $8890 + $8400 + $7920 for each year respectively). Without using an equation, the program cost would be $40,000.

Sensitivity Analysis

Sensitivity Analysis: The major problem facing by a study of economic analysis is an uncertainty regarding the correct value used for a given cost or benefit or whether the correct discount rate was used. To eliminate this problem, a researcher comes up with sensitivity analysis.

For example if original analysis used a discount rate of 4% for calculating cost or benefit, than a sensitive analysis would use the range of discount rates (2 to 6%). For each discount rate, a sensitivity analysis would obtain cost or benefit and compare those values with the original analysis (4% discount rate).

If the difference between values obtained from the original analysis and sensitivity analysis is minor, a researcher would be confident that the discount rate used originally is the most appropriate. However, if there is a significant difference between the two values, a researcher should reevaluate the whole analysis method.

Types of Economic Analysis

There are five major methods to conduct economic analyses:

1. Cost of Illness Analysis
2. Cost Minimization Analysis
3. Cost Benefit Analysis
4. Cost Effective Analysis
5. Cost Utility Analysis

1. **Cost of Illness Analysis:** This type of evaluation method includes all costs and consequences related to treating a particular disease. It is really important to conduct Cost of Illness Analysis before initiating further economic evaluation.

Advantages of using Cost of Illness Analysis:

1. This method allows researchers to collect and assess disease specific data.
2. It provides a true definition of the particular illness.
3. It provides researchers information about epidermology and potential outcome of illness, and the consequences associated with the illness.

The perfect example of cost of illness study would be a large multicenter survey conducted to obtain data regarding healthcare utilization of people suffering from diabetes. This example represents the analysis that was conducted from the perspective of the healthcare provider. The types of costs included in this type of survey would be:

1. In-patient hospitalization costs
2. Home healthcare related services costs
3. Prescription costs
4. Long-term care costs
5. Outpatient visits costs

2. **Cost Minimization Analysis:** This type of analysis is used to examine the cost associated with two or more alternatives that are clinically equivalent in terms of outcomes.

Equivalency must be established before conducting an analysis. Furthermore, equivalency studies must include not only therapeutic outcomes but also the type of adverse effects associated with therapies. Cost minimization can be calculated by using the following formula:

Cost (dollars) of intervention A <, =, or > Cost (dollars) of intervention B

An example of cost minimization analysis would be the comparison of two treatments with the same drug but different routes of administration. In both cases, if the therapeutic outcomes as well as the incidence and type of adverse reactions remain the same, one should chose the less expensive and laborious route of administration of the drug.

3. **Cost-Benefit Analysis:** It is a type of study in which all costs, outcomes or consequences are expressed in monetary terms. This type of analysis is conducted when two competing therapies or programs have different outcomes. All costs and benefits related to both therapies are compared in terms of dollar value. The only disadvantage of this analysis is that it is very difficult to assign dollar values to therapeutic outcomes. For example, assigning a dollar value to quality of life or pain and suffering due to disease.

The following equation can be used for cost-benefit analysis:

1. Cost-Benefit Ratio = Cost ($)/Benefit ($)
2. Net Benefit = Benefit ($) - Cost ($)

The perfect example of cost-benefit analysis would be a small clinical institution with very limited financial resources to choose from one of two programs; each used to treat different diseases. In this type of analysis, the researcher shall compare all costs that may have incurred for each program verses benefits in terms of morbidities and mortalities. The program with more net benefit should be implemented.

4. **Cost-Effective Analysis:** In this type of analysis, costs and consequences (outcomes) are simultaneously measured-costs in monetary terms (dollar value), and consequences (outcomes) in terms of obtained unit of effectiveness.

This type of analysis differs from the cost-benefit analysis in that the therapeutic outcomes or consequences are measured in nonmonetary terms.

Cost-Effective Ratio = Cost ($)/Therapeutic effect (natural units)

An example of the cost-effective analysis would be treating hypertensive patients with two different drugs, drug A and drug B. Drug A reduces an average blood pressure by 20 mm/hg, and drug B lower an average blood pressure by 40 mm/hg. If both drugs cost the same, than drug B would be a better choice to treat hypertension.

There are two types of Cost Effective Analysis (CEA):

1. Classic CEA
2. Lifetime CEA

1. **Classic CEA:** In this type of CEA, the new treatment is compared with the standard treatment (usually, the best available treatment in clinical practice, e.g., the gold standard) in terms of clinical and economic value. If the treatment has just been launched on the market, and a study cannot be carried out in the practice setting, effectiveness data is obtained from published trials. In this situation, the most powerful trials (e.g., the one with the strongest methodology as well as with the largest number of patients) should be considered. An alternative would be to use the results of a meta-analysis comprising all the concluded relevant trials on the issue.

Using Pharmacoeconomic Analysis Study For Two Therapies For Formulary Decision

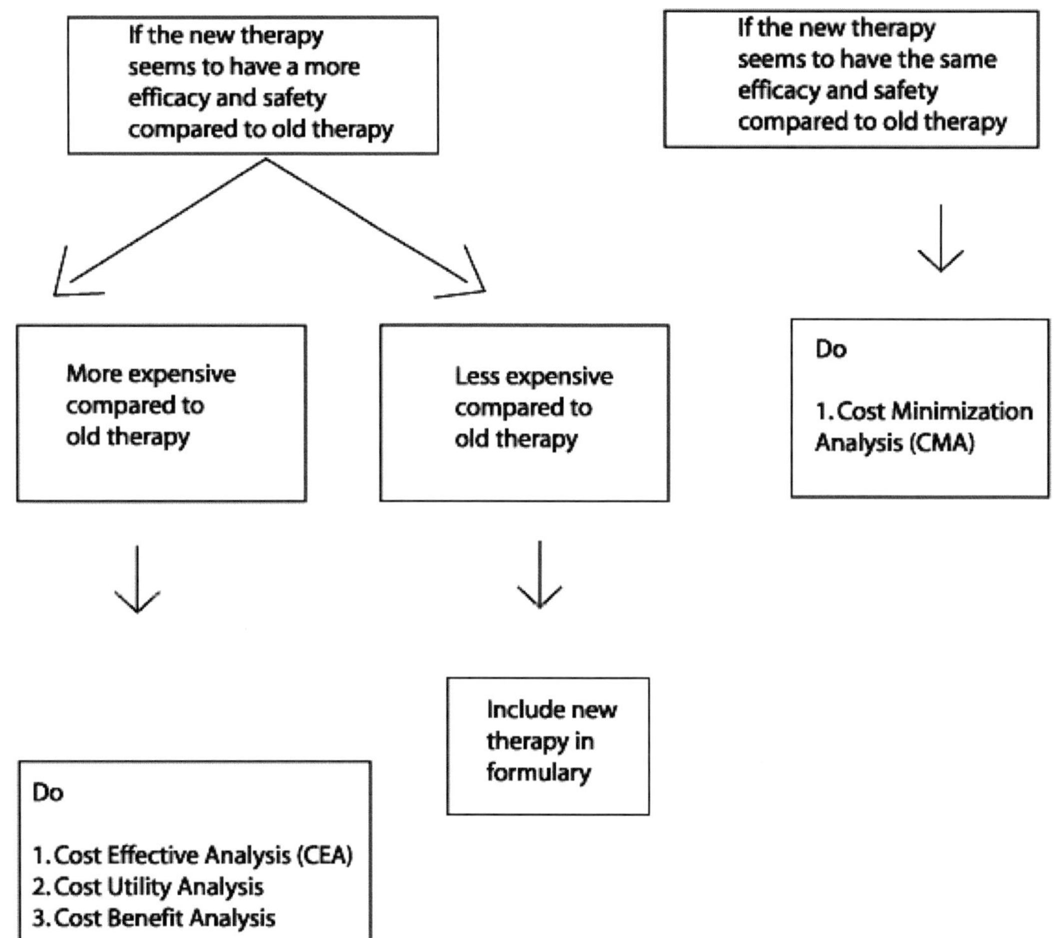

For example, one method frequently used is to normalize both costs and outcomes values for a hypothetical population of 100 patients. If, for instance, the costs of the new treatment A is $7,000 and the cost for treatment B is $3,000 for one year, the cost for 100 patients is $70,000 and $30,000, respectively.

Using the same methodology, if the new treatment A reduces the recurrence rate from 39% to 15% of the standard treatment B; this means that the new treatment avoids a total of 24 recurrences for every 100 patients. This constitutes the clinical benefit. It is important to point out that both costs and outcomes need to refer to the same time frame, in this example, one year. Finally, to calculate the CER, the ratio between incremental cost in the numerator ($40,000) and incremental benefit in the denominator (24 recurrences) is calculated. The result is about $1,700 spent for each avoided recurrence.

The above procedure is a very simplified example of short-term CEA over a one-year time period. The major simplification is the time frame considered. The choice of one year makes the calculation easier, but it excludes the contribution of significant events occurring later in the disease and treatment process, related to both costs and outcomes. Generally, these simplifications may be more or less acceptable, depending on the problem under the study.

2. **Life CEA:** Therapeutic problems which require long term efficacy evaluations often correspond to the use of a methodology which measures the survival length on a long- term basis and which synthesizes this data through life table curves. This methodology is largely applied in oncology.

The main difference between a classic CEA and a lifetime CEA is in the methodology of computing the benefit. The denominator is the gain in terms of survival (e.g., the incremental survival). Thus, the results of the CEA are expressed as cost per year of life saved. It is, in fact, demonstrated that the survival length of a group of patients may be determined by the calculation of the area under the curve of the actuarial survival curve as a function of time (AUC). The AUC value corresponds to the years of life (or patient-years or person-years) lived by the patients. The incremental gain in years of life is calculated from the difference between the two AUC values.

$$\text{Life Time CEA} = \frac{\text{Cost for treating 100 patients with Drug A} - \text{Cost for treating 100 patients with Drug B}}{\text{Years of Life Gained Using A Instead of B}}$$

The only disadvantage associated with Cost Effective Analysis is that one cannot compare two different outcomes. For example, one cannot compare therapeutic outcomes in mm/hg for treating hypertension with mg/dl of total cholesterol.

5. **Cost-Utility Analysis**: It is defined as a method where costs are measured in terms of dollar amounts and consequences are measured in terms of quality of life. Cost effective analysis and cost utility analysis are almost same, the only difference between them is the unit of consequences or therapeutic outcomes. The former measures the outcomes in natural units (e.g. reduction in blood pressure or blood glucose level) whereas the latter relies on quality-adjusted life years gain.

Cost-Utility Ratio: Costs ($)/Utilities (e.g. QALY, Quality Adjusted Life Years)

QALY is the number of years at full health compared to the number of years of illness. A year of perfect health would be calculated as 1.0 measured on QALY, and death would equal 0.

For example, six years of perfect health would be counted as 6.0 QALY, whereas six years of living with cancer, with each year having a utility of 0.4, would be valued at 2.4 QALY.

Now, utilities for a particular disease (in our example, it is cancer) can be calculated by the following methods:

1. Through Estimation
2. Through The Literature
3. Through Actual Measurement

Physicians, researchers or special panels can assign the utility value for a particular disease.

There are three instruments that help measuring utility values. These are:

1. Rating scale
2. Standard gamble
3. Time-trade off

The major advantage of a cost-utility analysis is that it is the only analysis method which calculates consequences or outcomes in terms of the quality of a patient's life. The only disadvantage associated with this method is a lack of uniform or standardized methods to calculate utility values for diseases.

13. Differential Analysis

Differential Analysis: It is a method of study in which a pharmacy can analyze the financial future of an organization if alternatives have been implemented. In simple term, it reveals how a new change in the pharmacy will affect its current business. For example, RX Care Pharmacy has an offer to join the NY-Third Party Prescription Program, which will offer their plan members prescription-related services.

If RX Care Pharmacy accepts this offer, it will bring an additional 1000 prescription per year to the pharmacy. The NY Third Party Prescription Plan proposes a flat fee of $3.50 per prescription to RX Care Pharmacy. Under these circumstances, the differential analysis shall help RX Care Pharmacy to make a decision as to whether accept an offer or not.

The only thing RX Care Pharmacy should be concerned with is that the $3.50 dispensing fee per prescription would it be sufficient to cover the pharmacy expenses (due to an increase in prescription volume) and generate reasonable profits?

To calculate whether a particular change may guide the business in a positive direction or not, three types of costs should be estimated. These costs are:

1. Differential Costs
2. Sunk Costs
3. Opportunity Costs

1. **Differential Costs:** These costs are expenses that may be incurred due to a new change applied to the pharmacy. For example, if RX Care Pharmacy accepts the offer presented by the NY Third Party Prescription Program, it will increase its yearly prescription volume by 1000. If the pharmacy has to hire more pharmacists or technicians to cover this additional volume, the cost related to this should be classified as the differential costs.

2. **Sunk Costs:** These are costs that have already been incurred. For example, RX Care Pharmacy joins Macke Wholesale Drug Groups, Inc., which offer a 10% discount on AWP with an annual registration fee of $10,000. Soon after joining Macke, RX Care Pharmacy finds another group which offers a 15% discount on AWP with an annual fee of $5000. In this scenario, the $10,000 which is paid to Macke Wholesale Drug Groups would be considered as sunk costs.

3. **Opportunity Costs:** These are hypothetical expense that may incur by using available resources for other services. For example, RX Care Pharmacy uses a small portion of the pharmacy space to educate and counsel patients. By providing this service, the pharmacy will earn a gross profit $20,000 per year.

If RX Care Pharmacy uses the same space to sell herbal products, it would bring a profit of $30,000 per year. Hypothetically, RX Care Pharmacy gives up an opportunity to earn $10,000, or loses $10,000 worth of business. Therefore, $10,000 would be defined as opportunity costs.

There are four important steps in conducting a differential analysis. These are:

1. Identifying Differential Revenues
2. Identifying Differential Costs

3. Calculating Contributional Margin
4. Considering Non-Quantitative Factors

We will use two sets of examples to explain this. In the first situation, assume that RX Care Pharmacy will gain 1000 prescriptions per year by accepting the NY Third Party Prescription Program.

The NY Third Party will pay the RX Care Pharmacy a flat fee of $3.50 per prescription. Using this data, differential revenue (DR) for RX Care Pharmacy would be:

DR = 1000 Rx x $3.50 = $3500

We will now calculate the cost that may be incurred due to increased prescription volume. Since the prescription volume of the pharmacy increased by only 1000 prescriptions per year, RX Care Pharmacy will not have to hire additional pharmacists or technicians. The pharmacy's manager anticipates that there will be a dollar cost per prescription. Therefore if dispensing 1000 prescriptions per year, the differential cost (CS) would be:

DS = 1000 Rx x $1.00 = $1000

Therefore, the contribution margin (CM) for RX Care Pharmacy would be:

CM = DR - DC
CM = $3500 - $1000
CM = $2500

Thus by accepting an offer from the NY Third Party Prescription Plan, RX Care Pharmacy will make net profit of $2500 per year.

In the second situation, assume that by accepting the NY Third Party Prescription Plan offer, the prescription volume of RX Care Pharmacy will increase by 20,000 prescriptions per year. Using the same reimbursement rate, the pharmacy differential revenue would be:

DR = 20,000 Rx x $3.50 = $70,000

Due to a large increase in prescription volume, the pharmacy has decided to hire two full-time technicians and one part-time pharmacist. The approximate costs to hire these new members would be $50,000 per year. Using the same cost of $1 per prescription, the total differential cost would be:

DC = $50,000 + (20,000 Rx x $1.00)
DC = $50,000 + $20,000
DC = $70,000

The new contribution margin would be:

CM = DR - DC
CM = $70,000 - $70,000
CM = $0.00

Therefore in this case, RX Care Pharmacy will not have any incentives if it accepts the NY Third Party Prescription Plan offer.

Considering Non-Quantitative Factors

Even though pharmacy does not perform well financially, a hospital administrator cannot make the decision to close pharmacy solely on the basis of financial situation. The administrator must take into account other non-quantitative factors.

For example,

1. It could be the only pharmacy that provides service in a neighborhood community.

2. The closing of the hospital pharmacy may affect the morale of other employees working in the hospital.

Decision Analysis

Decision Analysis: A technique used to aid decision-making under conditions of uncertainty by systematically representing and examining all of the relevant information for the decision and the uncertainty around that information. The available choices are plotted on the decision tree. At each branch, or decision mode, the probabilities of each outcome that can be predicted are estimated. The relative work or preferences of decision-makers for the various possible outcomes for a decision can also be estimated and incorporated in a decision analysis.

It is normally used to assist a decision maker to:

1. Identify the available option when faced with a decision.
2. Predict the consequences or outcomes of each question.
3. Assess the likelihood or probability of the identified possible outcomes.
4. Determine the value of each outcome.
5. Select the decision option that will yield the best result.

14. Instruments To Measure the Quality of Life

The Quality of Life is the therapeutic end point for all diseases and healthcare related procedures, since in the healthcare profession the thing that matters the most is the quality of life provided by healthcare resources.

The Quality of Life measuring instruments are divided into two major categories:

1. Disease Specific Instruments
2. Generic/General Instruments

A. Health Profile
B. Utility Based Instruments

1. **Disease Specific Instruments:** They provide detail information in terms of functioning and well-being that may be associated with the particular disease. They are classified into the following categories:

1. Disease Specific (e.g. hypertension, diabetes)
2. Population Specific (e.g. elderly, infant)
3. Function Specific (e.g. sexual functioning)
4. Condition or Problem Specific (e.g. pain)

Examples of Disease-Specific Instruments:

1. Arthritis Impact Measurement Scale (AIMS)
2. Asthma Quality of Life Questionnaires (AQLQ)
3. Diabetes Quality of Life (DQOL)
4. Functional Living Index Cancer (FLIC)
5. Quality Of Life In Epilepsy (QOLIE)
6. HIV Overview of Problems-Evaluation System (HOPES)

2. **Generic/General Instrument:** As the name suggests, general instruments put more emphasis on all conditions that have a general effect on quality of life. The general/generic instruments provide the better picture of disease or condition. The KDQOL (Kidney Disease Quality Of Life) is the perfect example of general/generic instrument, and it can be further explained by learning profile and utility-based instruments.

A. **Health Profile:** It provides important information on the quality of life or the health status of an individual. The principal advantage of health profile is that it provides multiple outcome scores which may be useful for predicting the effect of disease or treatment on an individual's quality of life. A commonly used profile instrument is the Medical Outcomes Study Short-Form 36 (SF-36). This instrument concentrates on the following areas:

1. General health perception
2. Physical functioning
3. Social functioning
4. Role limitations attributed to physical problems
5. Role limitations attributed to emotional problems
6. Bodily pain

7. General mental health
8. Energy/fatigue
9. Health transition

B. **Utility-Based Instruments:** These types of instruments measure the specific patient health states along with an adjustment for the preferences (e.g. utilities) for the health state. The preferences can be measured or assigned through the variety of methods; these methods are:

1. Visual Analog Scales
2. The Time Trade-Off Technique
3. Standard Gamble

The outcome scores of this type of instrument ranges from 0 to 1, and represents the quality of life associated with death and perfect health respectively. That's why utility based instruments are really important for conducting the cost-utility analysis since as discussed previously, the cost utility analysis measures the cost in a dollar amount and therapeutic outcomes in units such as quality-adjusted life years gain (QALYs).

QALYs gain measures both quantity and quality of life. This can be an important outcome measurement for the disease such as cancer where the treatment itself has the major impact on a patient's functionality and overall wellbeing. To better understand, we can take the following example. Let's say a patient is suffering from lung cancer. We want to find out and compare costs and therapeutic outcomes (QALYs) for two alternatives, one with surgery option and the other with surgery plus chemotherapy option. The patient will gain 3 years (unadjusted) of his life if he receives the surgery and adds chemotherapy agents in his regimen, however the Quality of Adjusted Life Year (QALYs) gain would be only 0.5 (since the addition of chemotherapy agents may increase patient's years of life however reduces his quality of life due to serious side effects of the drugs involved).

Now, let's compare the cost associated with both alternatives. If the patient's only receives the surgery, the calculated cost per life year gain would be $3000 whereas if he receives surgery and uses chemotherapeutic agents, the cost per QALY gained would be $20,000. Thus maximizing the potential of pharmaceutical care will require that pharmacists understand and be able to address the economic and quality of life implications of therapeutic decisions.

Examples of utility based instruments are the Quality of Well Being Scale (QWB), the Health Utility Index (HUI), and the EuroQol.

Quality of Life and Patient Satisfaction

Humanistic outcomes are closely related to individual attitudes and beliefs relating to health and health-related services. Therefore, it is very important to consider psychometric properties of instruments that are essential for the successful measurement of humanistic outcomes.

Psychometric Properties: Psychometrics refers to the measurement of psychological construct such as quality of life or patient satisfaction. It is generally associated with the development and testing of new instruments in such a way that we can have confidence in the result predicted by the instrument. Psychometric properties include the reliability and validity of measurements. These two properties (reliability and validity) have major impact on measuring humanistic outcomes.

Reliability: It refers to the consistency, stability and reproducibility of results. The extent to which we are measuring some attribute in a systematic and therefore repeatable way. For an instrument to be reliable its results must be reproducible and stable under the different conditions in which it is likely to be used. Reliability is decreased by errors of measurement. There are three methods by which the reliability of given instrument can be measured. These methods are:

1. Test-Retest Method
2. Internal Consistency Method
3. Inter-Rater Reliability

1. **Test Retest Method:** The only problem with the test-retest method is that this method will not serve the purpose of an experiment. Since we are measuring humanistic outcomes as our final product, it is really hard to apply this method. For example quality of life (humanistic outcome) is not going to remain constant over a period of time.

2. **Internal Consistency:** This method indicates the extent to which an instrument is free from making random error. The degree of internal consistency is indicated by coefficient alpha. It can be calculated by using Cronbach's Coefficient Alpha. Values above 0.90 are required for making comparisons between individuals, and above 0.50 are required for comparisons between groups.

3. **Inter-Rater Reliability:** The degree to which the measuring instrument yields similar results at the same time with more than one assessor.

Validity: It defines the range of inferences that are justifiable on the basis of measure. It also refers to the extent to which differences in test scores reflect the true differences in individuals under study. Three basic types of validity normally considered are:

1. Criterion
2. Content
3. Construct

1. **Criterion:** It is the degree to which a test predicts some criterion (measure of performance), usually in the future. To ascertain this kind of validity, evaluators look at the correlation between the test and the criterion measure. For example, a college admission test has criterion validity if it can predict some aspect of college performance (e.g., grades, degree completion).

2. **Content Validity:** This refers to tests such as skills, ability or attainment tests where the domain of items is much defined. A test with good content validity represents and samples adequately from the curriculum or content domain being tested. This kind of validity involves logical comparisons and judgments by the test developers rather than the specific statistical technique. For example, a high school biology test has content validity if it tests knowledge taken from biology textbooks assigned to students and reinforced by teachers in their instructional program.

3. **Construct Validity:** This refers to whether a test is measuring what it claims to measure as judged by accumulated evidence. A variety of statistical techniques can be used to see if the test behaves in ways predicted by the given construct. For example, a new test of computer programming skills would be expected to correlate highly with other valid tests of computer skills. Conversely, this new test would be expected to have little correlation with a different type of test (such as a test of social intelligence).

15. Pricing Strategy for New Products

There are many different types of pricing strategies are available for selecting prices for new products to achieve the optimum sales. But we will discuss only a few of them.

1. Skimming Pricing Strategy
2. Penetration Pricing Strategy
3. Cost Plus Pricing Strategy
4. Competition-Based Pricing Strategy
5. Parity Pricing Strategy

1. **Skimming Pricing Strategy:** It is a type of strategy in which initially a high price is set for a new product to "skim the cream" off the upper end of the demand curve. This strategy is recommended when a company spends a big chunk of money in developing and researching a new product. This strategy is also recommended when the demand of the new product is uncertain and the competition is expected to develop in the near future.

To decide how high a skimming price should be, the company has to concentrate on the following factors:

A. Chances of competition entering the market: If competitors are expecting to introduce new products in the near future, it would be advisable to keep the skimming price high, and if competitors are years behind in introducing new products, the low skimming price would be more useful.

Price elasticity at the upper layer of the demand curve may also affect the new product skimming price.

2. **Penetration Pricing:** This pricing strategy is designed to achieve sales-based objectives. It is the strategy to enter into the market with a low initial price so that greater shares of the market can be captured. High price elastic demand is the most important reason for adopting the penetration strategy. This strategy also discourages competitors to enter into the market due to a lower profit margin.

3. **Cost-Plus Pricing:** It is a price fixing strategy in which predetermined profit is added to the cost of the product to determine the product's selling price. The price can be calculated by using the following formula:

P = (AVC + FC %) x (1 + MK %) where,

P = Price
AVC = Average variable cost
FC% = Percentage allocation of fixed costs
MK% = Percentage markup

The problem facing this method is that profit is expressed as a percent of the cost, and not as a percent of the sale. Another difficulty with this method is that the price is not related to demand. For example, if there is a high demand for a particular product in the market, the company that uses this method to calculate the price would not be able to take advantage of more profit by setting the price higher in accordance with demand.

4. **Competition-Based Pricing:** There are companies who use competitor's prices rather than the product's cost or demand. A company may set prices below the market, at the market, or above the market depending on customers, image, consumer loyalty and the company's reputation.

5. **Parity Pricing:** The product is priced equivalent to the prevailing price levels in the market. It is the most common approach used by firms launching products into already established markets.

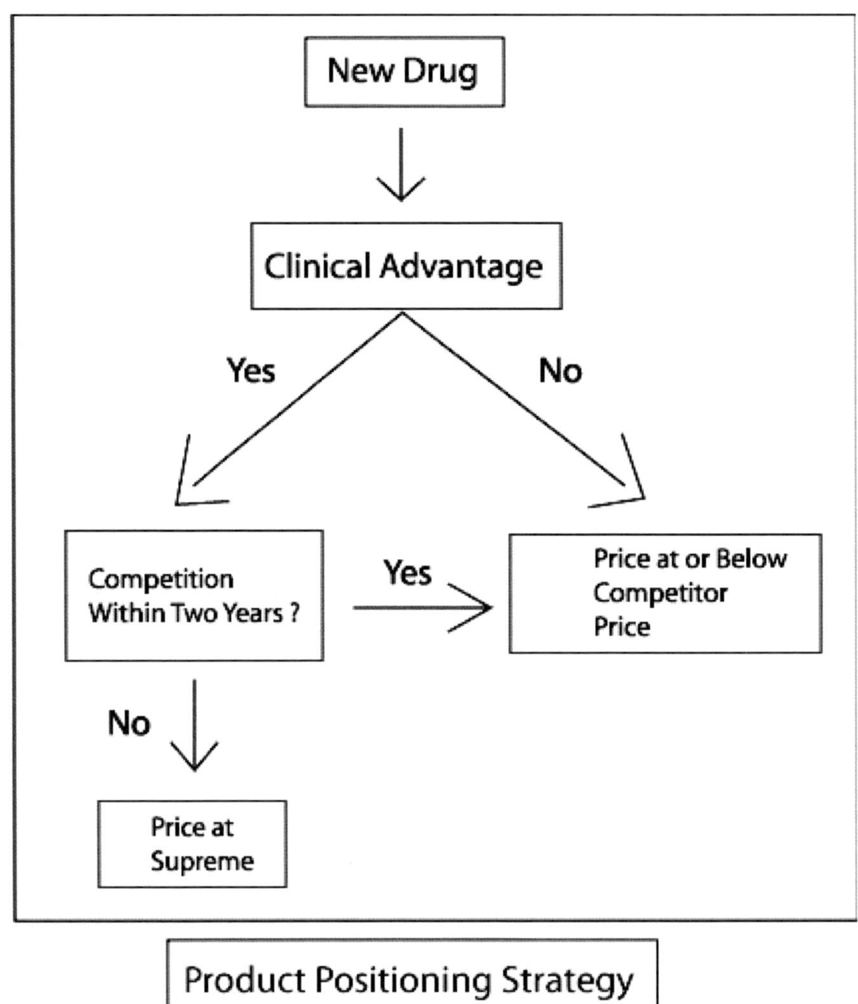

Product Positioning Strategy

The "positioning" refers to placing a product in a particular area of the market where it will be most likely to receive a favorable reception compared to competing products.

Since the market is heterogeneous, it is very important to place the new product in the right segment of the market. One should also try to attempt to place a product so that it stands apart from competing brands.

Positioning also helps to highlight the product from other competitive brands. It tells what the product stands for, what it is, and how the consumer should evaluate it.

Positioning strategy can be subdivided into the following segments:

1. Attribute Positioning
2. Price/Quality Positioning
3. Use/Application Positioning
4. User Positioning
5. Product Class Positioning
6. Competition Positioning

Product Repositioning Strategy

Very often, a product may require repositioning. This can be occured if:

1. The product has been initially placed into the wrong positioning.
2. Another product in the market may enter into the market next to the product, and may adversely affect the market capitalization of an existing product.
3. The product original preferences have been changed.
4. New preferences have been discovered which may open the door for new opportunity associated with the product.

Costs and risks associated with repositioning are really high. To avoid these risks, one should use the technique of perceptual mapping to evaluate and justify product repositioning. Perceptual mapping helps examining the position of product relative to competing products.

Product Elimination Strategy

Marketers have believed that products that do not perform well should be eliminated. When a product reaches the stage at which continued support can no longer be justified because its performance falls short of expectations, the product should be pulled out of the market.

A product can be removed from the market if:

1. It has a low profitability.
2. There is a profound decline in sales volume or market share that would be too difficult to build up.
3. A product may enter into a mature or declining phase of the cycle.
4. A product may have a risk of technology obsolescence

There are three alternatives in the product elimination strategy. They are:

1. Harvesting
2. Line Simplification
3. Divestment

1. **Harvesting:** It refers to getting the most from the product while it lasts. This strategy is applied to a product or business whose sale volume and market share are slowly declining. It leads to a slow decline in sales.

Harvesting strategy should be used when the following conditions are present:

1. The product is in a stable or declining market.
2. The product has a very small market share which is very costly to build up.
3. The product has a respectable market share but it is very expensive to maintain or defend at the current position.
4. The product is not producing a good reasonable profit to even cover the cost of production.
5. The company has better uses for the freed-up resources.

2. **Line Simplification:** It refers to a situation in which a product line is trimmed to a manageable size by adjusting the number and variety of products or services being offered. It is a defensive strategy. It is especially useful during times of rising costs and resource shortages.

The principal advantages of line simplification are:

1. Potential cost savings from longer production runs.
2. Reduced inventories.
3. Helps shifting concentration to do aggressive marketing, R & D, and other efforts to the shorter list of products.

3. **Divestment:** It is a situation of reverse acquisition. This strategy is used by companies to get rid of the product that is not doing well even in a growing market. It is an aspect of product strategy. With the advent of strategic planning, divestment became an accepted option for companies looking for faster growth. More companies are believed to sell the business if the company will be better of divestment.

Demand and Elasticity of Demand

In today's market, a company can significantly increase its revenue by utilizing the concept of elasticity of demand.

Elasticity of demand is defined as an indicator that measures the effect of price changes on the quantity demanded of given commodity. Elasticity of demand can be classified into five different categories:

1. Perfectly Elastic Demand
2. Elastic Demand
3. Unit Elasticity of Demand
4. Inelastic Demand
5. Perfectly Inelastic Demand

1. **Perfectly Elastic Demand:** When the price change of the product may result in an infinite change in the quantity demanded, it is classified as perfectly elastic demand.

2. **Elastic Demand:** When the price change of the product may result in greater than proportionate changes in the quantity demanded of product, it is defined as an elastic demand.

3. **Unit Elasticity of Demand:** When the price change of the product may result in an exactly proportionate change in the quantity demanded of product, it is defined as unit elasticity demand.

4. **Inelastic demand:** When the price change of the product may result in less than proportionate changes in the quantity demanded of the product, it is defined as an inelastic demand.

5. **Perfectly inelastic demand:** When the price change of the product does not have any effect on the quantity demanded, it is defined as perfectly inelastic demand.

Coefficient of Elasticity: The coefficient of elasticity can be calculated by the following formula:

E = Q/P Where E = coefficient of elasticity
Q = the relative change in quantity expressed as a percentage
P = the relative change in price expressed as a percentage

Example: If we reduce the price for Tolnaftate cream from $3 to $2.80 and this will increase the sale of Tolnaftate tubes from 55 to 85 tubes, what would be the coefficient of elasticity?

Q = The relative change in quantity as a percentage = (85-55)/55*100 = 54.54%

P = The relative change in price as a percentage = (2.8 – 3)/3*100 = -(6.66)%

E = Q/P = 54.54/-(6.67) = -8.17

Price Elasticity of Demand (PED Or Ed) is a measure used in economics to show the responsiveness, or elasticity, of the quantity demanded of a good or service to a change in its price. More precisely, it gives the percentage change in quantity demanded in response to a one percent change in price.

Price elasticities are almost always negative, although analysts tend to ignore the sign even though this can lead to ambiguity.

In general, the demand for a good is said to be inelastic (or relatively inelastic) when the PED is less than one (in absolute value): that is, changes in price have a relatively small effect on the quantity of the goods demanded.

The demand for the good is said to be elastic (or relatively elastic) when its PED is greater than one (in absolute value): that is, changes in price have a relatively large effect on the quantity of goods demanded. When Ed = 1, it is considered a unitary elasticity.

In the current market of prescription drugs, we face most situations with inelastic demand. Changes in price on prescription drugs may not result in proportionate inverse changes in the quantity demanded. Since prescription drugs are used for health purposes, it is unlikely to see a low demand of prescription drugs, even at high prices. This causes inelastic demand.

This is possible since prescription drugs (products) are useful for health purpose and therefore patients will not compromise their health with pricing of prescription drugs.

The other factor that also affects the inelasticity of prescription drugs is the influence of physicians. Patient will give secondary consideration to price over physician's decision. The other categories will rarely be seen in today's market. Among these all, the type of elasticity least likely to be found within the current market would be perfect elasticity.

16. DRGs (Diagnosis Related Groups)

DRG: It is known as diagnosis-related groups. **Diagnosis-Related Groups (DRGs)** are a classification of hospital case types into groups expected to have similar hospital resource use. Medicare uses this classification to pay for inpatient hospital care. The groupings are based on diagnoses, procedures, age, sex, and the presence of complications.

Under this form of payment, the hospital is paid the specific amount for each patient treated, regardless of the number or types of services provided. Thus, the hospital is rewarded for reducing the cost of treating a patient over the entire course of the hospital stay. Per case payment removes the incentive to provide more technologies and encourages the hospital and its physicians to consider explicitly the benefits of additional services against their added costs. It helps cut down the healthcare costs. It is the choice of payment for most third party payers. The reimbursement under DRG is considered Prospective Reimbursement.

Under DRG-payment method, medical problems are classified and the amount to treat each particular disease is pre-calculated. For example, MS is admitted to the Adecare Hospital for coronary bypass surgery.

Under DRG, the cost (including surgery, patient's stay in hospital and medications) for this particular medical problem is $65000. Third party insurance companies are going to pay only $65000 to Adecare Hospital regardless of the service provided.

This discourages the hospital from keeping MS in the hospital more than required. Now, if the actual cost to treat MS's medical condition comes to $72000; Adecare Hospital shall pay the difference ($7000) from its own pocket. Similarly, if the actual cost comes to $53000, Adecare Hospital will make an additional profit.

However, per-case payment under this method is not as simple as it looks since the system does not take into account other factors that may affect the hospital's reimbursement and quality of care. For example, if hospitals were paid the same amount for each admission regardless of its clinical characteristics, over time they would be encouraged to treat patients who are less ill and avoid the cases that require more resources. Therefore, it is required to conduct and evaluate the study which can also take into account these other important factors, normally known as "Case-Mix."

Case-Mix has been defined as the relative frequency of admissions of various types of patients, reflecting different needs for hospital resources. There are many ways of measuring Case-Mix; some based on patient diagnoses or the severity of their illnesses some on the utilization of services, and some on the characteristics of the hospital or area in which hospitals are located.

Diagnosis Related Groups (DRGs) are just one of several approaches for measuring the hospital Case-Mix. In recent years, their importance is increased because the Medicare Prospective Payment System have approved them. Because Medicare is willing to accept DRGs and use them as basis for hospital reimbursement programs, an evitable need arises to set up an organization that can verify, justify and evaluate DRGs and their structures. For this reason, the Office of Technology Assessment (OTA) was requested by the House Committee on Energy and Commerce and its Subcommittee on Health and the Environment to examine DRGs and their implications for use in the Medicare program.

This study of evaluating DRGs is also known by Diagnosis-Related Groups and Medicare Program. It examines the validity and reliability of the DRG classification system, the accuracy of DRG coding, and the administrative feasibility of administering the DRG-based payment system. It provides examples of proposed and actual uses of

DRGs in hospital pay merit. Finally, the technical memorandum includes a thorough analysis of the implications for medical technology use and adoption of using DRGs as an integral part of a per-case payment system. This analysis includes the review of the key features of design of DRG payment systems that affect medical technology, and the discussion of the implications of technological change for the administration of DRG payment system over time.

Managed Care Organizations (MCO)

17. Managed Care Organizations

Managed Care: It is defined as a system of health care delivery that influences or controls the utilization of services and costs of services.

Due to the rising cost of healthcare, the federal government proposed the HMO act in 1973. The major goal was to control the health care spending and utilization services.

The principle features of the HMO act are:

1. Feasibility grants and low-interest development loan programs made available to encourage interested parties to develop and build an HMO.

2. The establishment of procedures through which health plans could become "Federally Qualified HMO."

3. Inclusion of preventive as well as curative health care benefits.

4. Requirements that employers offer federally qualified HMOs to their employees under certain circumstances.

What is an HMO?

Health Maintenance Organization is the health care payment and delivery system involving networks of doctors and healthcare institutions. It offers consumers a comprehensive range of benefits at one annual fee (often with copayments or deductibles that vary from service to service) but they can see only providers in the network. Physicians and other health professionals often are on salary or contracted with the HMO to provide services. Patients are assigned to a primary care doctor or a nurse as a "gatekeeper" who decides what health services are needed and when.

The HMO members receive comprehensive preventative, hospital, and medical care from specific medical providers who have agreed upon pre-set rates. Members select the Primary Care Physician or medical group from the HMO's list of affiliated doctors, and generally have no deductibles or claim forms. Members make the small copayment, usually between $3 and $20. Some HMOs have capitated contracts with providers and some pay providers on a single discounted fee-for-service basis.

An HMO can be classified into four major models:

1. Staff Model HMOs
2. Group Model HMOs
3. Network Model HMOs
4. IPA Model HMOs

1. **Staff Model HMOs:** In this type of HMO, physicians are employed by facilities that are owned and operated by HMOs. Major services such as diagnosis, laboratory tests, and pharmacy services are provided on-site. Many staff model HMOs also own hospitals.

   Staff model HMOs have the high control over costs and utilization of services since physicians and other healthcare providers are employees of HMOs.

Pharmacy services are provided by on-site pharmacies established by staff model HMOs. To better serve and increase patient's compliance, they also contract with local, chain and mail order pharmacies to provide prescription services.

2. **Group Model HMOs:** These types of HMOs contract with multi-specialist physician groups practices to provide healthcare related services to their plan enrollees.

Under the group model HMOs, physicians are employees of the group practices and are restricted to provide services to only the HMO's enrollees.

There are two kinds of group model HMOs.

A. The first type of group model is called the **Closed Panel**, in which medical services are delivered in the HMO-owned health center or satellite clinic by physicians who belong to the specially formed but legally separated medical group that only serves the HMO. The group is paid the negotiated monthly capitation fee by the HMO, and the physicians are salaried and generally prohibited from carrying on any fee-for-service practice.

B. In the second type of group model, the HMO contracts with an existing, independent group of physicians to deliver medical care. Usually an existing multispecialty group practice adds a prepaid component to its fee-for-service mode and affiliates with or forms the HMO. Medical services are delivered at the group's clinic facilities (both to fee-for-service patients and to prepaid HMO members). The group may contract with more than one HMO.

An example of the group model HMO would be the Kaiser Permanente Health Plan. Like staff model HMOs, the group model HMOs also provide the most pharmacy related services on-site and sometimes through chain or mail-order pharmacies.

3. **Network Model HMOs:** In this type of HMO model, the HMO contracts more than one multi-specialty physician group to provide and cover wide geographical areas.

Pharmacy-related services are again provided by in-house pharmacies, chain pharmacies and mail order pharmacies.

4. **IPA model HMOs**: This type of HMO does not have its own medical facilities. They normally contract with independent community-based physicians and group practices.

They also contract with hospitals to provide other medical facilities (e.g. lab tests or diagnostic services).

Unlike other HMO models, they don't have any in-house pharmacies; however they contract with chain and mail-order pharmacies to provide pharmacy related services to plan enrollees.

Other Managed Care Organizations

Managed healthcare also provides healthcare-related facilities through organizations other than HMOs. The following is a list of such organizations:

1. PPOs

2. POS
3. EPOs
4. PHOs

1. **PPOs:** Also known as Preferred Provider Organizations. They are a contracted network of hospitals and physicians (by an insurance carrier) that provide healthcare related services similar to HMOs.

They differ from traditional HMOs in following ways:

1. They provide a larger network and more freedom of choices (providers) to patients compared to traditional HMOs.

2. They are more expensive than traditional HMOs, but less expensive compared to indemnity insurance.

3. They exert less control over providers (physicians, hospitals, pharmacies) than HMOs.

2. **POS:** A hybrid of PPO and an HMO. The members of a POS plan can obtain healthcare services through an HMO or a PPO network. The members who select HMOs shall pay lower monthly premium compared to members who select the PPO network. However, the member who selects the PPO network has a more freedom of choice in selecting physicians and health-related services over the members of traditional HMOs.

3. **EPOs:** They are similar to PPOs but members can only use contracted providers. For example, Dr. Brooke is not a contracted provider of an EPO; a member cannot use this physician for health-related services. EPOs are normally established by large employer groups to achieve the goal of cost containment.

4. **PHOs:** They are known as Physician Hospital Organizations. They are owned by hospitals and affiliated physicians. They also contract with traditional HMOs to provide their members to access large geographical areas.

Physicians Reimbursement Methods

Physicians associated with different types of HMOs are usually reimbursed by the following mechanisms:

1. Salary
2. Bonus Associated With Plan Performances
3. Capitation
4. Discounted FFS Arrangements

Among these, the Discounted FFS Arrangements and Capitation Reimbursements are the most commonly used methods to reimburse the physicians by HMOs.

A. **Capitation Reimbursement:** In this type of reimbursement, a physician or a group of physicians will receive a fixed monthly fee for providing healthcare-related services to assign members.

Under this reimbursement method, physicians will receive the same monthly fees per member regardless of patient's' visits or services provided by physicians.

This method discourages physicians from providing unnecessary medical services to patients in order to earn more financial incentives.

Under this monthly per capita payment, a capitated physician is expected by plan sponsors to cover the full range of services such as outpatient visits, preventive care, diagnostic and laboratory tests, etc.

B. **Discounted FFS Reimbursements:** Under this type of reimbursement, physicians receive payment when they provide covered services to plan enrollees. However, their reimbursements are discounted from U & C reimbursement rates. In addition, physicians will receive the portion of reimbursement, often 80%. The remaining 20% is withheld by plan sponsors and paid out at the end of the year only if certain performance objectives are met.

Physicians who do not perform efficiently or in other words are costly do not receive 20%. Physicians who are moderate to average performers will receive their reserve withheld (20%). Physicians who perform exceptionally well and are least costly will receive their own (20%) as well as a portion (20%) from the physicians who do not perform efficiently or who are costly.

Types of Reimbursements for Managed Care Prescription Plans

Manage care prescription plans are reimbursed through the following methods:

1. Capitated Reimbursement Method
2. fee-for-service Reimbursement Method

1. **Capitated Reimbursement Method:** As discussed earlier, under this type of reimbursement method, a pharmacy will receive a fixed monthly fee for the number of members associated with the plan regardless of services. Under the capitated plan, the pharmacy will receive the reimbursement from two major sources:

1. Fixed Monthly Capitated Rate Per Plan Member
2. Copayment Fee Prescription Dispensing

$$\text{Total Reimbursement} = \begin{matrix}\text{Capitation fixed}\\ \text{monthly fees}\end{matrix} \times \begin{matrix}\text{No. of plan}\\ \text{members}\end{matrix} + \begin{matrix}\text{Amount of}\\ \text{Copayment}\end{matrix} \times \begin{matrix}\text{No. of RX}\\ \text{dispensed}\end{matrix}$$

Advantages:

1. Under this plan, pharmacies are getting fixed monthly premiums from plan sponsors and therefore they have less incentive to fill unnecessary prescriptions. This may help the plan sponsors cut down and control the prescription costs.

Disadvantages:

1. Due to the fixed monthly rate, pharmacies are at high risk for costs and utilization of services over which they have very limited control.

2. **Fee-for-service Reimbursement Method:** There are three major factors that may affect the fee-for-service prescription plan method.

1. Unit costs
2. Utilization rates
3. Administrative costs

Under this plan, total prescription costs can be calculated by the following equation:

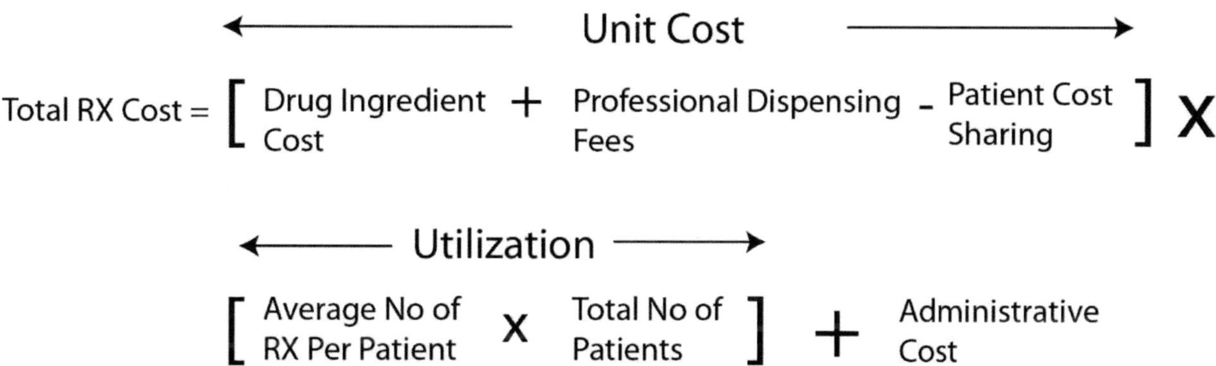

1. **Unit Costs:** It is the sum of drug ingredient costs and professional dispensing fees. This sum is reduced by any amount that is contributed by the patient out of his/her own pocket.

   The cost of drug ingredients is normally reimbursed on the basis of AWP or Average Acquisition Wholesale Price. This AWP is normally 15% higher compared to AAC or Actual Acquisition Cost. The difference between AWC and AAC is known AWP Differential or Earned Discount.

   The AAC is completely dependent on the pharmacy's purchasing volume, inventory turnover rate, and ability to negotiate with pharmaceutical manufacturers. Since the AAC is highly variable and difficult to interpret due to the above mentioned factors, health care plan sponsors usually reimburse pharmacies on the basis of calculated EAC or Estimated Acquisition Cost. An EAC is normally calculated on the basis of AWP, and is generally 90 percent of AWP.

2. **Dispensing Fees:** The professional dispensing fee is designed to cover the pharmacy's overhead expenses plus the reasonable net profit. There are a few manage care plans that are experimenting to increase professional dispensing fees as an incentive for pharmacies in order to provide more cognitive services from them.

3. **Utilization:** The utilization costs of a managed care plan can be calculated by multiplying the average number of prescriptions per patient (intensity) by the total number of patients enrolled in the plan (populations).

$$\text{Utilization} = \left[\begin{array}{l}\text{Average No of}\\ \text{RX Per Patient}\end{array} \times \begin{array}{l}\text{Total No of}\\ \text{Patients}\end{array} \right]$$

4. **Administrative Costs:** The expenses that are incurred by managing pharmacy benefit program are defined as administrative costs. This also includes the expenses that are incurred when contracting with the PBM. Most HMOs and other managed care plans handling PBM programs have asked participating pharmacies to submit claims electronically in order to reduce administrative costs and to increase work efficiency. Also, most HMOs and PBMs link their point-of-sale system to participating pharmacies in order to prevent over-utilization, to ensure formulary compliances, and to screen pharmacy claims before final submission. This can save a lot of time and administrative cost which could be incurred due to claims rejection or resubmissions.

Discounted FFS Reimbursement Chart:

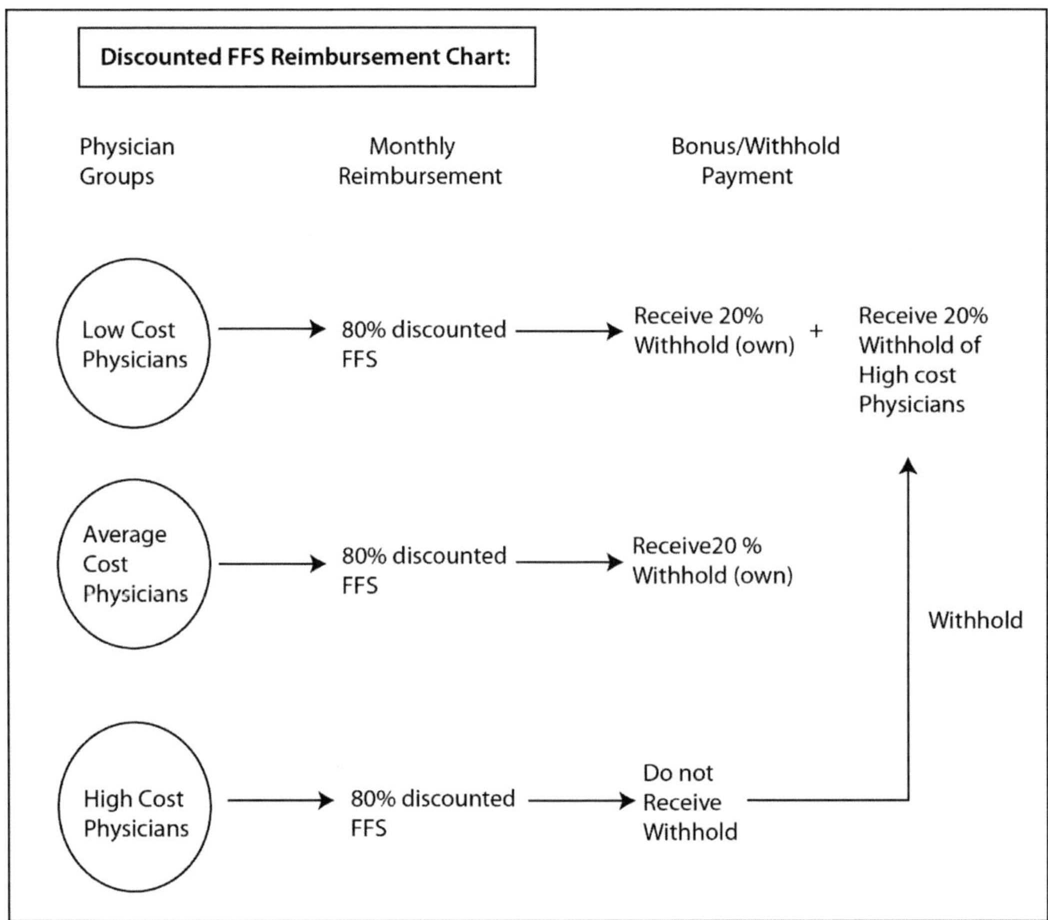

Medical Loss Ratio (MLR)

Medical Loss Ratio: It is defined as the cost of providing actual healthcare divided by the premium received from the plan members. To better understand this term, look at the following chart.

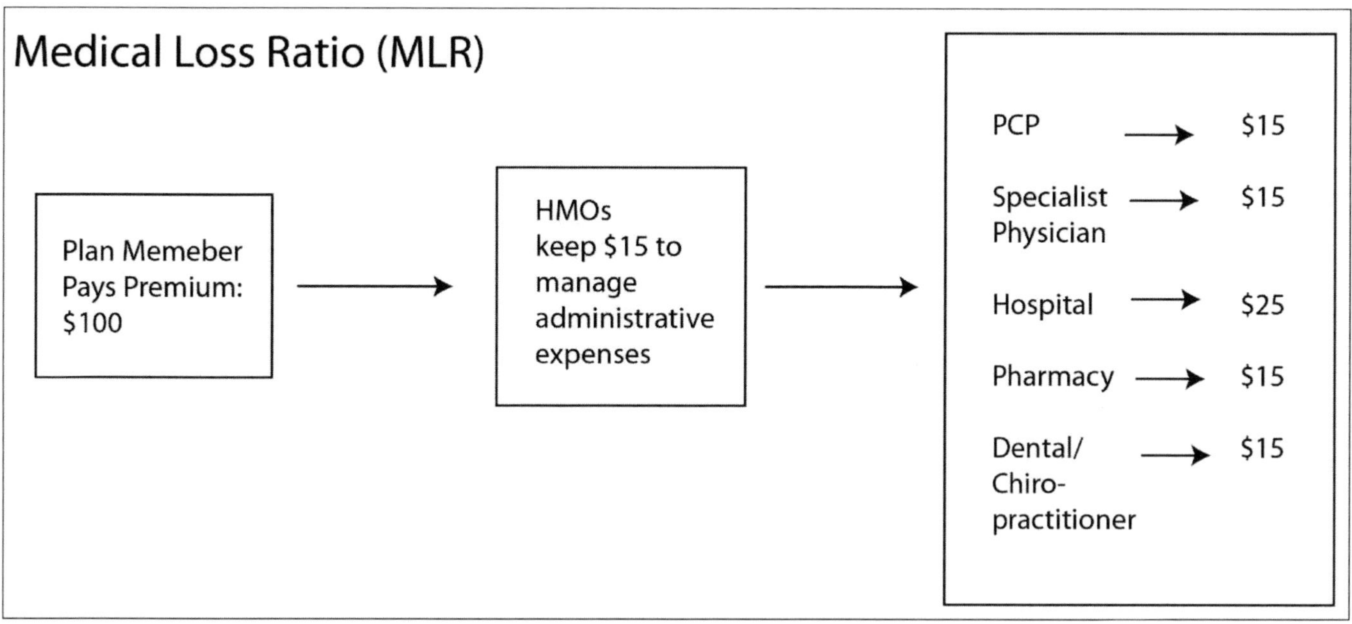

In the above example, the MLR ratio would be:

$$\text{MLR Ratio} = \frac{\text{Cost of Providing Healthcare}}{\text{Premiums}}$$

$$\text{MLR Ratio} = \frac{85}{100} = 0.85$$

0.85 is known as the MLR ratio. Generally, employers are looking for higher MLR ratios since the higher MLR suggests more of the premium is paid to cover the premium costs rather than retained by the HMO as management fees. The MLR is useful to find health-related benefits and evaluated the efficiency of the health plan.

Measurement of Quality Care in Managed Care:

Patients purchasing healthcare services may expect high-quality healthcare. There are three important elements that should be kept in mind to get a proper picture of the healthcare provided. These elements are:

1. Structure
2. Processes
3. Outcomes

1. **Structure:** It is defined as the building block of quality healthcare. It establishes the foundation of healthcare. For example, pharmacists must have proper guidelines or criteria before dispensing drugs.

2. **Process:** It normally evaluates procedures to obtain optimum therapeutic outcomes.

3. **Outcomes:** They normally measure the long-term impact of the process (element) on the quality of healthcare.

<u>There are a few organizations that are involved with quality measurements of managed care. These include:</u>

1. National Committee for Quality Assurance (NCQA)
2. The Joint Commission on Accreditation of Healthcare Organization (JCAHO)
3. The American Accredited Healthcare Commission (AAHC)
4. The Foundation for Accountability (FACCT)
5. The Agency for Healthcare Policy and Research (AHCPR)

18. Pharmacy Benefit Management (PBM)

There are two important factors that affect the overall costs of healthcare. They are:

1. Cost Per Unit Of Service
2. Number Of Units Utilized

Managed Care Organizations (MCOs) control these costs by controlling the supply and demand of healthcare-related products and services. The supply side controls involve physicians, pharmacists and pharmaceutical manufacturers.

In order to obtain effective supply side control, an MCO tries to buy or reimburse drug and dispensing fee-related services at a discounted price. Demand side controls involve patients. This can be achieved by introducing copayments or coinsurances whenever plan members obtain healthcare services. This way the MCO eliminates unnecessary visits to physician offices or pharmacies, and keeps healthcare costs under control.

In order to create effective supply side control, the MCO has initiated to provide pharmacy benefits through their own internal pharmacy departments or through carve-out pharmacy management organizations which are specialized in pharmacy related services. This gives a birth to Pharmacy Benefit Management (PBM).

Most carve-out PBMs were created within internal pharmacy departments of large HMOs. However, there are two exceptions: Prescription Card Service (PCS) and Merck-Medco did not originate from HMOs. They started as independent pharmacy benefit management providers.

Most managed care prescription drug benefits include the following areas of services:

1. Provides a defined physician's network
2. Provides a defined pharmacist's network
3. Provides a list of drugs covered under formulary
4. Provides a mandatory generic substitution program
5. Offers a retrospective DUR study
6. Offers a prescription copayment plan

In order to successfully market pharmacy benefits, PBMs must consider the formula of the four "Ps": Products, Price, Place, and Promotions.

Medicare Pharmacy Benefits

State Medicaid and Federal Medicare regulations are the biggest challenges for PBMs and MCOs to control health-related costs. As these regulations are continuously updating, both, MCO and PBM are facing even more difficulties.

As Medicare programs offer a very limited drug benefit coverage, a managed care plan that offers an optional drug benefit coverage are at the top, and most popular among the Medicare-Eligible population. These types of plans help senior citizens to get their medications at reasonable prices and support compliance and persistence with the prescription therapy.

Also, by promoting and supporting elderly prescription medication needs, these types of managed care plans can even save the large amount of healthcare expenditures every year related to drug noncompliance. For example, reduced emergency hospitalization costs in senior patients by increasing and encouraging drug utilization in older patients.

Medicare Pharmacy Benefits costs can be controlled by the MCO following ways:

1. By limiting the annual-benefit-maximum or cap. It ranges from $500 to $2500 per year. This way, health plan sponsors can restrict a single member from depleting the funds that cover the benefits of many other plan members.

2. By providing a closed formulary. The formulary guides the members to use more cost effective drugs without compromising the quality of care.

3. By providing mail-order pharmacy services. It offers unique benefits to the Medicare risk program. The principal advantage of mail-order pharmacy services are convenient home delivery, and a 90-day supply of the drug for the cost of just one copay.

MCOs also offer plan members the option to select the level of benefits by offering different copayment rates.

Medicaid Pharmacy Benefits

Most states participate in a cost-controlling strategy for the Medicaid program. This can be achieved by contracting with health plans, PBMs, and other MCOs. By transferring the financial burden of the state Medicaid program to MCOs or PBMs, states can reduce the drug-related costs and increase the overall efficiency of Medicaid programs.

Pharmacy benefits of Medicaid programs may not be limited to prescription drugs services. Many benefits include durable medical equipment, adult diapers, non-prescription drugs, prosthetic devices, diabetic supplies, etc. To successfully obtain the Medicaid state contract, a MCO or PBM has to include all the mentioned benefits in their proposal.

Unlike Medicare, the Medicaid program does not have any benefit cap. The program also offers a few copayments based healthcare plans to its enrollees.

Pharmacy Benefit Design

As we all know, prescriptions drugs will continue to be an important element for controlling total healthcare costs. Drugs developed to be selective and effective for specific diseases with fewer side effects will be increasingly in demand by payers and plan members, however these more "focused" drugs are going to be more expensive than less selective drugs within the same class. This is going to be the main concern for pharmacy benefit design.
A PBM (Pharmacy Benefit Management) that offers more selective drugs with reasonable prices are likely to be favored by payers and plan members. However, there are a few other factors which will also affect the pharmacy benefits design for PBMs and other health plan sponsors. These factors are:

1. An inclusion of lifetime enhancement drugs in pharmacy benefits.
2. A provision of electronic prescribing by the prescriber in pharmacy benefits.

1. An inclusion of lifetime enhancement drugs in pharmacy benefits:

The release of new pharmaceutical drugs that are designed to improve the quality of life or extend the normal life span have a tremendous response from payers and plan members, and therefore the inclusion of such products in pharmacy benefit design are required by PBMs and other health care plan sponsors.

2. A provision of electronic prescribing by the prescriber in pharmacy benefits:

A provision of electronic prescribing by the prescriber in the pharmacy benefits design is the second major factor for selecting PBMs or other healthcare plans by plan members or payers.

Also, the PBM that develops a system which has the capability to identify the least expensive and most qualified drugs by prescribers (electronically) before prescribing will likely get more contracts, since members or plan members will not have any psychological effects of restrictive formulary.

In other words, electronic prescribing will eliminate the step of looking into drug-formulary, since physicians will consider side effects, effectiveness and the cost of drugs before prescribing drugs.

Pharmacy Distribution Systems

A successful Pharmacy Benefit Management (PBM) program will require a well-organized and efficient pharmacy distribution system. The pharmacy distribution systems help patients to access the most clinically appropriate and cost effective medications. From the patient's point of view, convenient access to the participating pharmacy providers is foremost.

These are three major options for the pharmacy distribution system:

1. Community Pharmacy Network Services
2. In-house Pharmacy Services
3. Mail-order Pharmacy Services

1. **Community Pharmacy Network:** It is a group of licensed community independent or chain pharmacies that have contracted with the health plan or PBM to provide services to their members.

2. **In-house Pharmacy Services:** They are usually located within the staff or group model HMO. These pharmacies only provide services to their HMO members.

3. **Mail-Order Pharmacy Services:** The third distribution option is the mail order pharmacy service. Very often, this option is included with the community pharmacy network.

Community Pharmacy Provider Network:

There are four basic types of community pharmacy networks:

1. Open, Pre Contracted or Shelf
2. Restricted, Preferred or Customized

3. Exclusive or Closed

4. Specialized

1. Open, Pre contracted or Shelf: This type of network will enroll any pharmacy that agrees to terms and conditions of PBMs or other healthcare providers.

Since the base reimbursement rate is inversely proportional to the size of the network, open networks usually have the highest reimbursement rates and program costs.

2. Restricted, Preferred or Customized: This type of network is designed to meet the needs of an individual plan sponsorship with a limited pharmacy network. The reimbursement rates and costs are lower than open pharmacy networks.

3. Exclusive or Closed: The closed or exclusive type of network has fewer pharmacies than restricted, preferred or customized pharmacy networks, and therefore has the lowest reimbursement rates and program costs.

4. Specialized Network: It is created to accommodate the specific class or types of drugs. Examples of such networks are HIV-related drugs, drugs for multiple sclerosis, interferon, etc. The specialized network service requires in-depth knowledge of the particular disease, patients' monitoring and therapeutic consultations.

The pharmacy participating in the specialized network must maintain an inventory of specialized medications or injectables. Reimbursement rates are based on product costs and the time necessary to provide the speciality service.

Advantages of Community Pharmacy Network:

1. Broad access to pharmacy services and covers large geographical areas
2. Quality pharmacy services
3. Administrative uniformity

2. In-House Pharmacy Services: In-house pharmacies are often associated with the staff model HMO, however sometimes you may also see them operated and owned by an employee benefit manager, a large employer (e.g. Walmart) or any location with a large number of plan members.

Advantages of In-House Pharmacies:

1. The principal advantage of staff model HMO in-house pharmacy is that it has the significant control over the physician's prescribing patterns.

2. Pharmacists and physicians work together to develop and prepare a drug formulary, which results in better compliance and cost-effective therapeutic outcomes.

3. A stronger working relationship between pharmacists and physicians.

4. Easy to integrate pharmacy-related data with medical data which helps improving member satisfaction.

5. Better and effective utilization of generic drugs by pharmacies.
6. Easy way to conduct and incorporate educational programs and other techniques that improve a

patient's awareness toward disease and improve therapeutic outcomes.

Disadvantages:

1. The major disadvantage of in-house pharmacies is their limited pharmacy network, which may not offer easy and convenient access to pharmacy services to its plan members.

2. The other disadvantage associated with in-house pharmacy services is a noncompliance; if the pharmacy is far away from the member's residence, the plan members may not be able to fill or refill prescriptions in a timely manner.

3. Mail Order Pharmacy Services

Most employers and plan members want mail-order prescription services along with retail and in-house pharmacy services. Mail-order pharmacy services have two distinguishable advantages:

1. Low copayment cost (usually 90-day supply per copayment)
2. Convenient delivery of medications

Other advantages associated with Mail-Order Pharmacy Services:

1. Administrative costs can be minimized by acquiring only one mail-order pharmacy location that serves as a central pharmacy to serve patients' prescription needs. Moreover, unlike retail pharmacies, mail-order pharmacy services do not require the commercial location since patients will receive the prescription in the mail.

2. Mail-order pharmacies normally fill ten times more prescriptions than average retail pharmacies. This gives them the benefit of wholesale discounts.

3. Since patients receive their medications through the mail, this would be the perfect option for disabled and elderly patients.

4. The average 90-day supplies minimize the dispensing time for pharmacists and technicians, and offers the better copayments rates.

5. Many mail-order pharmacy services also offer a refill reminder service, which increases the patient compliance.

Disadvantages:

1. Lack of personal touch and face to face counseling.

2. Increased waste, with an average 90-day supply; there is a potential for waste if the medication is discontinued or changed by the prescriber.

Drug Formulary

A drug formulary is defined as a list of drugs that are covered by specific healthcare plan administrators. It can be subdivided into four major categories:

1. Open Formulary
2. Closed Formulary
3. Limited or Restrictive Formulary
4. Negative Formulary

1. **Open Formulary:** It covers almost all medications that are available in the market. Physicians who follow the open formulary can prescribe virtually any drug. Payers or plan members have to pay higher premiums due to freedom of choice.

2. **Closed formulary:** It is an exclusive list of specific drugs that may be covered under the health plan. This formulary restricts prescribers from prescribing drugs outside of the formulary. Drugs that do not appear on the list of approved products are defined as non-formulary drugs and are not covered by health plans or PBMs. A patient has to pay out of his own pocket in order to get non-formulary drugs.

3. **Limited or Restricted Formulary**: Limited, restricted, intermediate, partially closed, or selectively closed formularies are formulary hybrids. They restrict or limit the prescriber choices in certain therapeutic categories and offer unlimited choices within the remaining drug classes. An example of such a drug would be Finasteride for the treatment of male pattern baldness. A healthcare plan may opt out the whole category from the prescription plan.

4. **Negative formulary:** It includes a list of drugs that cannot be prescribed within a specific therapeutic class.

Formulary and Its Decision Making Process

The Pharmacy and Therapeutic (P&T) committee is the major decision making body for the formulary. It consists of physicians, pharmacists, and sometimes nurses. The physicians who are appointed on the committee often represent a wide scope of medical practices ranging from primary physicians to physician specialists.

The main focus of the committee is to develop policy and educate healthcare professionals on various aspects of healthcare-related subjects. As far as development of policy is concerned, most policies are related to evaluate and select drugs to be included in the formulary. The P&T committee also develops other policies pertaining to drug therapy to ensure safe and cost-effective drug therapy.

The members of the P&T committee are a team of local "drug experts", and may also serve as drug educators. They often help health plan managers and sponsors to make decisions regarding inclusion of new prescription drugs in the program.

The P&T committee also develops educational programs which guide their professional staff about appropriate drug therapy and drug usage. Many managed care organizations now put more emphasis on advice and decisions taken by their P&T committee. For example, just recently the P&T committee of a number of managed care organizations has developed and introduced educational programs on appropriate use of antibiotic therapy.

Under this program, a few guidelines are provided for healthcare professionals to ensure that antibiotics are dispensed to those cases (meet guidelines) that are the most clinically appropriate. Not only that, the program also educates patients not to expect antibiotic prescriptions all the time. Ultimately, patient care is improved with a reduction in antibiotic resistance cases, and cost effectiveness can be achieved by avoiding unnecessary utilization of expensive drugs.

The P&T committee most commonly relies on peer-reviewed clinical literature and information from the pharmaceutical manufacturer when evaluating a new drug. However, guidelines for evaluation of drug formulary submissions are now being developed by the Academy of Managed Care Pharmacy. These guidelines ask for data, regarding drug utilization costs and the impact of the drug on disease management, from pharmaceutical manufacturers in order to justify a drug's inclusion in the formulary.

Before introducing a new pharmaceutical product in the formulary, the P&T committee may review the following factors associated with the new drug product.

1. Source of supply and reliability of manufacturer and distributor
2. Unlabeled use and its appropriateness
3. Bioavailability data of the new drug
4. Pharmacokinetic data of the new drug
5. Pharmacological and pharmacodynamic properties of the new drug
6. Dosage ranges by route and age
7. Risk versus benefits regarding clinical efficacy and safety of a particular drug relative to other drugs with the same indication
8. Side and toxic effects profile of the new drug
9. Special monitoring or administration requirement of the new drug
10. Pharmacoeconomic data of the new drug
11. Cost comparisons against other drugs available to treat the same medical conditions

Drug Utilization Review

Drug Utilization Review (DUR): It is an ongoing study of the frequency of use and cost of drugs from which patterns of prescribing, dispensing and patient's use can be determined.

Advantages of DUR

1. To identify drug-drug interaction
2. To prevent therapeutic duplication
3. To prevent under- or over-dosing of medications
4. To improve the quality of care
5. To encourage physicians to use more formulary and generic drugs

The DUR process can be subdivided into three major categories:

1. Retrospective DUR
2. Prospective DUR
3. Concurrent DUR

1. **<u>Retrospective DUR:</u>** This type of DUR study is normally conducted after the drug therapy has already been administered. For example, studying sulfa hypersensitivity reactions in a patient received Glyburide.

Advantages of Retrospective DUR study:

1. It is very simple and easy to implement.

2. Study requires very limited resources.

3. Provides valuable information about future drug therapy.

Disadvantages:

1. The major disadvantage of Retrospective DUR is that it does not provide an immediate benefit to the patient's care. Since this study is conducted after an event has happened, there is no chance for change or to modify drug therapies.

2. The study is completely depending on written documentation filed in a patient profile which is often too insufficient to conduct the study or missing valuable information.

A Retrospective DUR study helps to identify:

1. Drug-drug interactions
2. Proper dosage of the drug
3. Over- and underutilization of therapy
4. Over- and under-duration of therapy
5. Abuse or misuse of drugs
6. Therapeutic duplications

2. **<u>Concurrent DUR:</u>** This type of DUR study is conducted at the time of dispensing drugs to patients. The study ranges from identifying potential drug interactions to therapeutic duplication of drugs. For example, a pharmacist dispenses a drug to a patient in a retail pharmacy setting.

Advantages of Concurrent DUR:

1. May prevent adverse or toxic outcomes of therapy.

2. May offer more control over a patient's care compared to a retrospective DUR study.

3. May prevent over- and underutilization of medications.

4. May prevent incorrect dosing

5. May alert a healthcare provider with pregnancy precaution drugs.

6. May prevent drug interactions and offer a drug-age precaution.

Disadvantages:

1. To identify and resolve drug-related problems under concurrent DUR studies is more complex and time consuming compared to the retrospective DUR.

3. Prospective DUR: This type of DUR study is normally conducted before dispensing drugs to patients. For example, physicians use the electronic prescribing to prescribe drugs.

Advantages:

1. Problems may be identified and resolved before the patient receives medication.

Disadvantages:

1. May require immediate access to a patient's information.

A Prospective DUR study helps to identify:

1. Drug allergy reactions
2. Drug-drug interactions
3. Drugs that should be avoided in certain disease conditions (e.g. liver cirrhosis, kidney failure)
4. Incorrect dosing
5. Therapeutic drug duplication

19. PBMs Performance Indicators

PBMs performance indicators are useful to find out how a PBM is managing a prescription benefit program. The following are financial indicators that are used to evaluate the PBM plan performance.

1. Per Member Per Month Cost (PMPM Cost)
2. Per Member Per Month Utilization (PMPM Utilization)
3. Average Prescription Cost
4. Generic Utilization Rate
5. Percent DAW Prescriptions
6. Percent Formulary Compliances

1. **PMPM Cost:** It can be calculated by dividing the total claims cost for prescriptions for a month by the number of covered members for the same month.

$$\text{PMPM Cost} = \frac{\text{Total claims cost for prescriptions per month}}{\text{Total number of covered members indicator per month}}$$

PMPM cost is most often used to evaluate the overall financial performances of the PBM. A few PBMs evaluate PMPM cost by considering different variables such as age, sex, or illness. However, when evaluating the financial performance of the PMPM, a few PBMs don't include certain claims that are expensive due to terminal illnesses such as cancer, HIV, brain tumors, etc. The reason not to include these types of claims in financial evaluation is to avoid the costs burden on other members of the healthcare plan.

PMPM ratio is normally affected by the following factors:

1. Cost of medications
2. Pharmacy network discount
3. Percent generic use
4. Copayment fee structure

Each factor may affect the PMPM cost, both directly and indirectly. For example, if the copayment rate is high, it will provide more benefit to the health plan (directly) and also discourage unnecessary use of medications by an individual due to the high copayment rate; thus it affects the PMPM cost indirectly.

2. **PMPM Utilization**: It can be calculated by dividing the total number of prescriptions filled in a given month by the total number of covered members for the same month. This ratio helps determining how the change in utilization may affect the total prescription costs.

PMPM utilization is affected by the following factors:

1. Age of plan members
2. Drug advertising by media directly to consumer
For example, as the age of a plan member increases, the rate of utilization will also increase.

3. **Average Prescription Cost:** It is the total prescription costs divided by the total number of prescriptions dispensed. This ratio allows the user to find out how brand name drug or generic drug utilization may affect the total costs of the healthcare plan.

An average prescription cost is affected by the following factors:

1. Inflation
2. Economy
3. Prescription utilization
4. Cost of medications
5. Generic utilizations
6. Manufacturer's discount policy

4. **Generic Utilization Rate:** It can be calculated by dividing the total number of generic prescription claims dispensed by the total number of prescription claims. The percent of generic is always less than 100 since there are always patent-protected brand names on the market.

A percent generic utilization rate is affected by the following factors:

1. Pharmacists
2. Prescribers
3. Advertising
4. Copayment fee structure of health plan

5. **Percent DAW Prescriptions:** It is the total number of prescriptions dispensed with DAW or "Dispensed As Written" divided by the total prescription claims.

A percent DAW is affected by the following factors:

1. Prescribers
2. Copayment fee structure of health plan
3. Patients' psychology

6. **Percent Formulary Compliance:** It can be calculated by dividing total number of prescriptions filled by using the formulary recommendation by the total number of prescription claims.

A percent formulary compliance rate is affected by the following factors:

1. Prescribers' incentive if they follow formulary
2. Pharmacists' incentive if they follow formulary

20. Growth of Pharmacy Benefit Management (PBMs)

PBMs are classified as the type of business entity that develop and manage prescription drug benefits for managed care organizations, for government programs such as Medicare and Medicaid, and for their staff insured employers.

There are three major groups that own or use the PBM services to provide prescription related services to their plan members. They are:

1. HMO, PPO, POS, insurance career
2. Medicaid, CHAMPUS, Federal Employer Benefit Program (government sponsored program)
3. Large companies that manage their employees' benefits (e.g. Walmart)

When an HMO, PPO, POS or any self-insured employer group cannot use their own pharmacy benefit program efficiently, they should approach the PBM service providers to increase the plan efficiency and reduce costs.

PBMs are originated through one of two distinct channels:

1. As independent companies
2. From within HMOs

The following are examples of a few PBMs that originated or were created from HMOs.

	HMO	Generated PBM from HMO
1.	United Healthcare	Diversified Pharmaceutical Services (DPS)
2.	Blue Cross Blue Shield of Maryland	Advance Program (AP)
3.	Prescription Care	Prescription Solution (PS)

The question arises that if HMOs are capable and efficient enough to run their own internal pharmacy programs, then why would they need the PBM's help? The major factor that drives the growth of PBMs is their large scale operation. A large size HMO, PPO or POS may manage at the most one million members, but PBMs manage over 10 to 50 million members. Due to the large scale of operation, they are more capable of negotiating with pharmaceutical companies and other healthcare- related entities to bring down cost, yet at the same time provide satisfied and quality services to plan members compared to an independent HMO, PPO or POS. This is the major reason for the overwhelming growth of PBMs.

Advantages of using PBMs over internal pharmacy management programs provided by an independent HMO, PPO, or POS:

1. By using a PBM service, managed care organizations (HMO, PPO, POS) can save program development costs, and system and real estate investment related expenses.

2. A PBM will provide more efficient service compared to managed care organizations due to their large pharmacy networking and manufacturer's contracts.

21. Medicaid and Pharmacy Benefit Management (PBM)

Medicaid was first established by the federal government in 1965. It is Title XIX of the Federal Social Security Act.

1. It provides services to medically indigent people.

2. The program is operated by individual states, although regulations, guidelines and policies, and interpretations are provided by the federal government.

3. Each state Medicaid agency determines its own benefit design and expenditure according to its annual budget. Individual states normally provide their Medicaid services through the specific government department or agency, often called the department of public health and welfare.

4. All state operated Medicaid services are provided by both the federal and state government. The specific ratio of funding from each source depends on the state (income), and ranges from 50 to 83%.

5. The more wealthy states with higher per capita incomes may receive less funding from the federal government for Medicaid.

People who are eligible to receive Medicaid benefits are classified into one of the following categories:

1. People whose benefits are mandated at the federal level.

2. People whose benefits are determined by the state level.

3. Infants born to Medicaid eligible women.

4. Children under age six whose family income is below 133% of the federal poverty line.

5. Individuals who are "medically needy" and going through expensive medical treatments, even though they do not qualify for Medicaid due to low-income criteria provided by Medicaid.

Under Medicaid, the following services are mandatory at the federal level:

1. Physician services
2. Inpatient and outpatient hospital services
3. Prenatal care
4. Laboratory X-ray services
5. Vaccinations for children
6. Family planning services and supplies
7. Rural health clinic services
8. Skilled nursing facility services

The following services are not federally mandated but if states provide these services, they will receive federal matching funds for providing these optional services:

1. Diagnostic services, clinic services, prosthetic device related services
2. Transportation, rehabilitation and physical therapy related services
3. Prescription, optometrist and eyeglasses related services

According to the federal government, the state shall emphasize four basic criteria when providing Medicaid benefit services. These include:

1. Each covered service under the plan must be sufficient in amount, duration and scope to justify the successful therapeutic outcomes. For example, if the recommended therapy to treat community acquired pneumonia requires a 21 day regimen of Amoxicillin, and if the state Medicaid programs cover only a 7-day supply of medicine, then the state Medicaid program does not meet the federally required criteria, and therefore is ineligible to receive the help from the federal government.

2. The state must not arbitrarily restrict or limit benefits that discriminate individuals on the basis of medical diagnosis or disease.

3. The state must apply its Medicaid services to the whole geographical area of the state.

4. The state must provide its recipients a freedom of choice that allows recipients to obtain services from any enrolled or participating providers.

Medicaid Reimbursements

Most states normally contract with MCOs on the capitation fee basis to provide services to Medicaid recipients. For example, Maryland State may contract with the RX Care organization to provide medical benefits to Medicaid recipients where the RX Care organization shall receive the flat fee of $150 per month per member regardless of the service taken by Medicaid recipients.

However, under this fixed monthly capitation fee structure, the RX Care organizations have to provide all medically necessary services to Medicaid recipients.

Most states normally fix the capitation fees based on prior claim histories; however fees may also vary because of other factors such as geographical region, provider service types, etc. Many times this capitation rate or fee may also include pharmacy services as part of medicaid benefits.

Many states now ask for prescription copayments for prescription related services. These copays may range from $0.50 to $3.00 per prescription, however even a small amount of copayment may restrict the patient from getting prescription benefits and result in larger expenses such as an emergency hospitalization expenses due to not taking medications. For this reason many states are now trying to eliminate copayments from their Medicaid plans.

The typical copayment reimbursement can be calculated by the following formula:

1. The dispensing fees generally range from $0.50 to $1.00 when managed care organizations (MCO) manage the Medicaid benefits, and may increase up to $3.00 when the state manages Medicaid plans on its own without the help of MCOs or PBMs.

2. In either case, participating pharmacies have to accept the given reimbursement rates by MCOs or PBMs even though the traditional Medicaid fee-for-service rates are higher than rates provided by MCOs or PBMs under state contracts.

3. A few plans also offer a variable dispensing fee structure. Under this type of reimbursement, the dispensing fees may vary by the number of prescriptions filled by a patient for a given month. For example, MS receives three prescriptions per month; the dispensing fee under the variable fee structure would be $3 for the first prescription, $2.75 for the second prescription, and $2.50 for the third prescription.

4. States may also be entitled to receive manufacturer's rebates from pharmaceutical companies under the Department of Health and Human Services and Federal Law. The discounted rate under such contracts may be set up to 15%. At the end of each quarter, states may submit invoices to each manufacturer with the detailed information about the specific product claims and utilization, and will receive 15% of the total cost of medications.

Current challenges facing State Medicaid Programs:

1. Freedom of choice laws
2. Overutilization and underutilization of medications
3. Medicaid fraud and abuse
4. Medicaid reimbursement policies
5. Medicaid eligibility criteria

1. **Freedom of Choice Laws:** This law allows Medicaid recipients to receive services from any physicians that participate in Medicaid programs. But, it is often seen that patients do not stick to the same physician for some reason, and may result in lack of coordination within the system and increased healthcare utilization costs.

2. **Overutilization of Medications**: There are patients who overutilized or underutilized pharmacy services provided by the state medicaid programs. The overutilization of prescriptions may increase the total costs of healthcare expenditures, while the underutilization of pharmacy services may result in unnecessary hospitalization, and subsequently raise the cost of healthcare.

3. **Medicaid Fraud and Abuse**: The State Medicaid programs are abused by providers and patients. Due to very limited financial resources; it is not possible for states to monitor providers' dispensing and prescribing patterns and patients' utilization trends by analysing claims. It has been found that many pharmacies fill unnecessary prescriptions in order to get more financial incentives from the Medicaid managed plan. In additions, physicians also prescribe unnecessary laboratory tests and other medical services for the same reason.

4. **Medicaid Eligibility**: State Medicaid programs may also face many difficulties in order to determine patient's eligibility to receive services under Medicaid programs. Many sociologists and cost analysis experts believe that Medicaid eligibility requirement guidelines set by the federal and state governments may discourage patients from getting healthy or seeking employment since this may disqualify them from receiving Medicaid benefits.

5. **Medicaid Reimbursement Policies**: Medicaid reimbursement policies have two opposite effects on two different components of the healthcare system. Many specialist-physicians do not provide these services to patients due to the low fee structure of the Medicaid plan. Also, physicians avoid the laboratory testing under the Medicaid plan due to a low reimbursement rate.

However, in regard to pharmacy services, the situation is different. Since Medicaid managed care plans pay the highest reimbursement rate for prescription related services than any other third party plans, most pharmacies have enrolled to provide pharmacy services to Medicaid plan members. This encourages timely refills by pharmacies in order to get financial incentives, and also increases patient's compliance with the therapy.

Current challenges for managed care organizations providing Medicaid benefits:

Managed care organizations providing Medicaid benefits through the state contract face the following challenges:

1. Lack of coordination of services and patients' medical data
2. Formulary restrictions
3. Medicaid recipient turnover rate

1. **Lack of Coordination of Services And Patient Medical Data**: This is the major challenge faced by managed care organizations. As previously stated, it is really difficult task to track down patients' health care utilization through Medicaid, since many patients do not stick to one primary physician, and there is no advance information system which can integrate all this data at one central location. This is the major challenge that affects the current healthcare expenditure as well as manages care efficiency to provide medical services to Medicaid recipients.

2. **Formulary Restriction**: It is another challenge that managed care programs are facing right now. According to federal and state pharmacy laws, managed care contracted through the state to provide medical benefits to Medicaid recipients must allow patients to access any drug that is approved and listed by federal and state laws under Medicaid services. This may affect the cost cutting strategy of managed care organizations since this may limit the list of drugs included in the formulary.

3. **Medicaid Recipient Turnover Rate:** It also affects the plan efficiency and health- related services provided by managed care organizations. Managed care plans seem more effective and efficient when a patient stays with the one health care plan for at least a year or more. Currently, Medicaid plans have an excessive Medicaid recipient turnover rate which has negative effects on both state Medicaid plans (traditional Medicaid) and managed care Medicaid plans.

22. Medicare and Pharmacy Benefit Management (PBM)

Medicare is the Title XVIII of the Social Security Act. It was first proposed in 1965. It provides medical coverage to people over 65 years of age. It is funded by the Health Care Financing Administration (HCFA). It provides services through two programs:

1. Medicare for physicians and hospital care
2. Patients under age 65 who have long-term disabilities or end-stage renal disease may also receive reimbursement from Medicare.

Benefits covered by Medicare:

Medicare benefits are divided into two major categories:

1. Hospital Insurance (Part A)
2. Supplemental Medical Insurance (Part B)
3. Medicare Advantage or Medicare + Choice (Part C)
4. Prescription Drug Benefit Programs (Part D)

1. **Hospital Insurance or Part A**: Individuals over age 65 who are eligible for Social Security benefits are automatically covered under this Part A benefit. The cost for Part-A Medicare is paid out from the Social Security fund. Part A covers the following health related services:

1. Inpatient hospital services
2. Nursing homes and home healthcare services
3. Hospice care services

2. **Part B or Supplemented Medicare Insurance:** It normally covers:

1. Physician services
2. Outpatient hospital services
3. Home health services which are not covered in part A
4. Services related to Durable Medical Equipment (DME)
5. An ambulance transportation fee

However, in order to receive benefits listed in Part B, the member needs to pay the small monthly fee, currently about $45. This premium covers the 25% cost of the total program cost, and rest is paid by the federal government.

Both Part A and Part B Medicare plans require deductibles and copayments from patients in addition to monthly premiums. Under the Medicare Part A, the patient must pay the first $800 out of his own pocket for the given year. Once the patient pays $800 deductible, the rest of the costs are shared by Medicare and the patient, depending on the plan agreement. Part B deductibles are $100 per year. Once patients pay this requirement, the rest of the costs are shared by Medicare and patients depending on the plan agreement. Currently, the coinsurance (once patients pay the $100 deductible) level is set for 20 to 50 percent depending on different plans provided by Medicare.

3. **Medicare Part C or Medicare + Choice**

Medicare Part C, formerly known as "Medicare+Choice," is now known as "Medicare Advantage." If the patient is entitled to receive Medicare Part A and enrolled in Part B, he/she is eligible to switch to the Medicare Advantage plan, provided that the patient resides in the plan's service area. Medicare Advantage provides the following options:

The introduction of the Medicare+Choice program represents what is arguably the most significant change in the Medicare program since its inception in 1965. As its name implies, the primary goal of the Medicare+Choice program is to provide Medicare beneficiaries with a wider range of health plan choices to complement the original Medicare option. Alternatives available to beneficiaries under the Medicare+Choice program include both the traditional managed care plans (such as HMOs) that have participated in Medicare on the capitated payment, as well as a broader range of plans comparable to those now available through the private insurance.

Option 1: **Medicare HMO:** This plan offers coverage under the Medicare HMO and is not necessarily new. Unlike other plans, this plan does not require the separate coverage or Medigap. As stated, Medigap costs vary by plan and state, but the monthly rate of $100 is not unrealistic. The major benefit from the Medicare HMO is the fact that there may not be any additional costs for care at all - since Medicare will cover everything. Detractors of HMOs point to the poor care, bad physicians, the requirement to use a limited number of specific physicians and so on. However, the more realistic and objective analysis tends to show good to very good approval ratings for HMOs overall. Additionally, one must recognize that private care by private physicians is not exempt from problems.

Under the current option, an enrollee has the right to opt out of an HMO and convert to standard coverage with only a 3-month notice. Starting in 2002, however, the required notice will be 9-month. This appears to be intent to stop frequent switching but it will unquestionably require a lot more research of the HMO that an enrollee selects since, if they opt for an unsatisfactory one, they will not be able to get out as quickly. This is part of the change in government and corporate philosophy in requiring more consumer involvement in making their own selections.

Option 2: **Medicare PPOs**: A Preferred Provider Organization is similar to an HMO with a network of physicians and hospitals that offer care at reduced costs to enrollees. They may use primary physicians as gatekeeper. The major differences between HMO and Medicare PPOs are:

1. Use any physician within the PPO network.

   OR

2. More importantly, pay a higher fee and opt to use the physician outside of the PPO network. (This format is now also being offered by some major HMOs).

Option 3: Provider Sponsored Organizations (PSO): Under this plan, hospitals and physicians will be able to form their own plans PSOs similar to an HMO. An article by the American Institute for Economic Research notes that an organization that involves such a small number of physicians and enrollees may be severely limited by finances and numbers to offer care at the same level of an HMO or PPO.

Option 4: **Medical Savings Accounts (MSA):** MSAs were introduced to the corporate world several years ago and have met with reasonable success. It offers enrollees (390,000 maximum) the ability to establish tax free savings accounts that are used mostly for medical expenses. These would be partially funded by Medicare based on the difference between what Medicare normally pays for beneficiary care and the cost of high deductible traditional hospital and major medical coverage for catastrophic care. The deductibles would be taken from the MSA balance. If there was an excess, the account could be withdrawn and used for other purposes. But if it was not sufficient, the enrollee would have to pay the difference. Essentially, there is the risk, if a patient is healthy and stays that way, he can come out ahead. However, if the patient is sickly and ends up with large medical bills, they would come out of his own pocket.

Option 5: Fee For Service: This is effectively what has been the "standard" for care for the past 20 years before the advent of HMOs. One is able to pick whatever physician he/she wants, but is also responsible for any costs beyond what Medicare allows. There are caveats to remember however. If you go back to the 80s, you can count the huge number of articles of how difficult it was to get a doctor who would accept Medicare payments. This is a most acceptable option if one has a lot of money, but if not, it could backfire against the bulk of the public if doctors left the Medicare system for the higher payments.

Option 6: This goes further in that Medicare would not even be involved with any medical coverage at all. The patient would contract directly with the physician to provide care.

The number of doctors might be limited; however Section 4507 of the Balanced Budget Act requires that any physician that does opt for this system will not be able to take Medicare patients for up to two years. Since so much medical care now covers the elderly, it is debatable how successful this option might become. But if too many doctors found it financially beneficial, may be all the "good" doctors would become private and the bulk of the citizenry would be left with the rest.

Medicare Fee-For-Service (2000): A private fee-for-service plan is private insurance program that charges enrollees a premium and cost-sharing amounts and lets beneficiaries choose the providers they want to see. No one knew if consumers would actually use the system. However, the First Medicare Private Fee-for-Service Plan is now approved in eight more states.

The U. S. Health Care Financing Administration approved a request by Sterling Life Insurance Company to expand private fee-for-service health care coverage to Medicare beneficiaries in eight states: Arizona, Delaware, Illinois, Iowa, Oklahoma, Pennsylvania, South Carolina and Washington on September 1. Earlier this year, Sterling Option 1 was approved to offer private fee-for-service health care coverage to Medicare beneficiaries in 17 other states. In most cases, beneficiaries enrolled in the private fee-for-service plan will pay less to see a doctor than under original fee-for-service Medicare.

4. Medicare Prescription Drug Plan (Part D):

The Medicare Prescription Drug, Improvement and Modernization Act of 2003 added Part D. Beginning January 1, 2006, Medicare beneficiaries purchasing optional part D will be able to get drug coverage through the separate drug insurance policy. If they are covered by a privately operated health plan that includes the prescription drug benefit, they would be ineligible for Part D.

Medicare Part D was projected to cost about $35 per month as a premium. If an eligible Medicare beneficiary puts off getting the Medicare Part D beyond the initial enrollment date, that individual will have to pay a higher premium. Medicare Part D will have a $250 deductible and will pay:

1. 75% of the first $2,250 spent
2. Nothing for the next $3,600 spent
3. 95% for drug bills over $5,850

The government would guarantee drug coverage in any region that does not have at least one stand-alone drug plan and one private health plan. Employers that offer equivalent drug coverage for retirees would receive tax-free subsidies.

Employers could also offer premium subsidies and cost-sharing assistance for retirees who enroll in Medicare drug plans.

Lower-income seniors and disabled individuals will receive additional help in paying for prescription drugs when the program starts in 2006:

1. People eligible for both Medicaid and Medicare will pay no premium or deductible and have no gap in coverage. They will pay $1 per prescription for generics and $3 for brand names (copays are waived for those in nursing homes).

2. People with incomes below about $13,000 ($17,600 for couples) in 2006 and assets of under $6,000 ($9,000 for couples) will pay no premium or deductible and have no gaps in coverage. They will pay $2 for generics, $5 for brand names, and nothing above the catastrophic limit.

3. People with incomes between $13,000 and $14,400 ($17,600 and $19,500 for couples) in 2006 and assets under $10,000 ($20,000 for couples) will pay premiums on a sliding scale, a $50 deductible and 15 percent of drug costs with no gaps in coverage. After spending $3,600 out-of-pocket in a year, co-pays will be $2 for generics, and $5 for brand names.

4. In the interim, Medicare recipients could buy the prescription drug discount card that the Department of Health and Human Services estimates will provide the savings of 10 to 25 percent off retail prices. Beneficiaries with 2004 incomes below $12,569 ($26,862 for couples) would get the drug discount card with a $600 per year benefit.

Medicare Modernization Act (MMA)

On December 8, 2003, President Bush signed the Medicare Prescription Drug, Improvement and Modernization Act (known as Medicare Modernization Act, or "MMA" of 2003.)

MMA will make a voluntary prescription drug benefit available for the first time to more than 400 million Medicare beneficiaries. In addition to offering the prescription benefit, the MMA is going to introduce the following new regulations:

1. It will add new preventive medical benefits for seniors.

2. It will make a wealthier seniors pay a higher monthly Part B premium for physician services.

3. In the area of pharmacy, it will change the way that Medicare pays for covered outpatient Part B drugs (i.e. immunosuppressants, oral cancer drugs, oral antiemetic drugs) and lower the reimbursement rates for Medicare durable medical equipment (DME).

4. The MMA will also create a national competitive bidding program for drugs and durable medical equipment starting in 2007.

5. This law also includes provisions that affect state Medicaid programs, under a new provision, and will create tax-free health savings accounts and increase the availability of generic medications to Medicaid recipients.

6. This law will also add the Medicare Part D prescription drug benefit program in 2006 and enable beneficiaries to enroll in national or regionally-based insurance plans that cover prescription drugs.

Medicare Approved Prescription Drug Discount Card Program

To provide Medicare beneficiaries, especially those without prescription coverage, with discount on their prescription medications, MMA establishes a Medicare approved drug discount card program.

All Medicare beneficiaries entitled to or enrolled in Medicare Part A and/or Part B, would be eligible for the Medicare-approved discount card (without any income limit).

The program will operate for the 18 month period beginning in June 2004, continuing through the end of 2005, to provide "interim relief" from prescription drug costs to uninsured Medicare beneficiaries before the Medicare Part D prescription drug coverage program begins in 2006.

The actual savings may vary; however the cardholder may save up to 10 to 25% on prescription medications dispensed through community and mail order pharmacies. The Medicare approved discount cards will have a Medicare-approved seal. Just as Medicare-approved discount cards are voluntary for beneficiaries; they are also voluntary for pharmacies. Individual, chain, and mail order pharmacies have been signing contracts and making business decisions about which discount cards they will and will not accept in their stores.
There are several criteria that card sponsors (i.e. HMOs, PBMs, etc.) had to meet before they could be approved by The Center of Medicare and Medicaid Service (CMS).

1. Drug card sponsors must have at least three years of experience in negotiating discounts with manufacturers and pharmacies and adjudicating claims, and must operate a program that serves at least one million.

2. Drug card sponsors have to provide discounts on covered drugs to all their enrollees, but they can vary discounts based on the type of enrollee or the pharmacy from which the covered drugs are obtained. They can also vary discounts by disease stage.

3. Drug card sponsors must provide convenient access to pharmacies, which means that the retail pharmacy network must be constructed so that 90% of beneficiaries in urban areas have access to a retail pharmacy within 2 miles.

4. Drug card sponsors must implement the system to reduce medication errors and prevent adverse drug reactions. Drug card sponsors must also provide enrollees with a card that complies with NCPDP standards, maintains a grievance process to resolve disputes, and is precluded from marketing non-drug products to Medicare beneficiaries.

Different Types of Medicare Programs

There were three major types of Medicare managed care plans (prior to 1998) based on the type of contract held with an HCFA.

1. Risk Contract Medicare Program
2. Cost Contract Medicare Program
3. Prepayment Plan

1. **Risk Contract Medicare Program:** It is the most popular among the given options. Under this type of Medicare program, an HCFA pays approximately 95% of the projected average annual per capita cost of service (AAPCC) to the Medicare HMO in the form of the per capita payment system.

The AAPCC number is normally calculated by government actuaries by estimating the total cost of medical services divided by the number of Medicare enrollees receiving services under the traditional fee-for-service Medicare system. Under this method, the contracting HMO assumes the full financial risks for all Medicare covered services. Depending on the county of service, the HMO may receive from $367 to $780 per member per month (PMPM).

2. **Cost Contract Medicare Program:** In this type of Medicare program, the predetermined PMPM cost is paid to the plan administrator based on the total estimated budget. At the end of the year, the difference between actual costs and the monthly payments are reconciled. Medicare recipients can obtain services outside the plan network without any restriction.

3. **Healthcare Prepayment Plan:** This plan is similar to cost-contract Medicare plans. The only difference is that this plan only covers Part B Medicare services (outpatient services, durable medical equipment services). Part A Medicare services such as inpatient hospital services, hospice care services, and home healthcare related services are not covered under this plan.

4. **Medicare Plus Choice:** This plan was introduced in 1997, and also known as Medicare Part C. Under this new payment plan, the plan sponsor is reimbursed at the rate of 95% of AAPCC.

Normally, Medicare beneficiaries prefer to join an HMO over traditional fee-for-service Medicare programs. The main reason behind this is that in certain counties, the reimbursement rates are so high that it may allow these HMOs to offer benefits beyond those benefits offered by traditional fee-for-service Medicare plans.

A Medicare recipient who joins the HMO may receive benefits which include dental coverage, eyeglasses reimbursement, hearing aids, reduced copayment fee structures, immunizations, health educations and many more.

A Medicare recipient who joins a traditional fee-for-service Medicare plan is also required to purchase an additional policy known as a MediGap policy in order to cover his out of pocket expenses. This policy costs around $1000 per year. However, if the Medicare recipient joins the Medicare plan offers through the HMO, he may not be required to purchase such a policy since Medicare-HMO provides services without any additional fee-for-services. Therefore, if the recipient joins the Medicare HMO plan over the traditional Medicare plan, he or she can save $1000.

To utilize prescription benefits more efficiently and economically, managed care pharmacy programs use the following strategies:

1. By improving the network of chain and independent pharmacies.

2. By addressing issues related with Drug Utilization Reviews (DUR).

3. By providing educational programs to patients through drug and disease literature or by face to face counseling.

4. By encouraging physicians and pharmacists to use more formulary drugs.

5. By encouraging patients to use mail order pharmacy services for maintenance medications.

23. Professions With Drug Prescribing Authority

Profession	Abbreviation	Remarks
Medical doctor	MD	As appropriate for disease related drugs
Dentist	DDS or DMD	As appropriate for dental related drugs
Podiatrist	DSC, PoD or DPM	As appropriate for extremities related drugs
Homeopathic	DO	N/A
Optometrist	OD	As appropriate for ophthalmic use
Veterinarian	DVM	As appropriate for animal only
Nurse practitioner	NP	Prescriptions need to be cosigned by supervising physicians
Physician Assistant	PA	Prescriptions need to be cosigned by supervising physicians
Chiro practitioner	DC	No prescribing authority

24. Electronic Prescribing and Its Outcomes

Electronic Prescribing (EP) is an EDI application that allows a physician to transmit a prescription order to a pharmacy online. Until now physicians cannot access the data at the time of prescribing drugs since they usually prescribe medications on prescription pads. Due to the recent advancement in the technology field, it is now possible for physicians to prescribe for patients through electronic prescriptions.

The most important advantage of EP is that it alerts physicians, before writing a prescription, to drug allergies, drug interactions, specific adverse reactions, inappropriate drugs for the indication, and much more, from previously stored data.

Advantages of Electronic Prescribing:

1. It reduces healthcare expenses by offering physicians the prospective DUR which may eliminate expensive emergency hospitalization.

2. It enables physicians to do online consultation.

3. It increases the efficiency of physicians.

4. It helps physicians to comply with drug formulary requirements since all data are available on computers.

5. Physicians can also access the patient's complete history through EP.

6. The EP system also alerts the physician to drug interactions, adverse reactions, redundant prescriptions, and incorrect dosing before the patient's leaves the physician's office, so that errors may be corrected before prescriptions go to the pharmacy.

7. Through EP, a prescription can be sent online or via fax, which gives pharmacists enough time to review prescriptions before dispensing to patients.

8. EP saves physicians' and pharmacists' time by providing "clean" prescriptions to the pharmacy. The word "clean" means the prescription is so clear that pharmacists are not required to call the physician's office to clarify prescriptions.

9. EP also reduces patient's waiting time in the pharmacy.

25. Disease Management Programs

Disease Management Program: It is considered to be a patient-focused, comprehensive approach to minimizing the treatment variability of a specific disease to improve patient care outcomes and optimize the expenditure of resources.

The main purpose to establish the disease management program is to:

1. Prevent illnesses
2. Avoid preventable exacerbations and complications
3. Reduce morbidity and mortality
4. Minimize the unnecessary use of resources
5. Reduce overall direct and indirect costs
6. Improve patient's quality of life
7. Advance physicians' knowledge of successful disease prevention and treatment

In the past, program sponsors (payers) have attempted to control the cost by focusing on individual components of the healthcare delivery system (e.g. hospitalizations, prescription benefits, laboratory tests services, outpatient visits), however no one ever thinks about controlling costs by preventing diseases at the first place. This program is inspired by the statement: "Prevention is better than cure."

The payers like the concept of the disease management program; however they are skeptical and unwilling to accept an unproven program that is expensive to implement. Also, the cost cutting strategy used by these plan sponsors made them unwilling to accept new changes in the delivery system. However, the problem arises when patients start to complain about too much emphasis put on cost cutting strategy, and there has been the constant decline in the quality of care. At this time, plan sponsors have started to think about other ways to cut down costs as well as improve the quality of care.

The disease management program attempts to apply principles of population based management for specific medical conditions to individual patients. Under this plan, physicians are encouraged to practice medicine using literature-based evidence that the treatment is cost effective when applied to patients with the same medical disorder or diagnosis.

There are certain criteria that must be met to include medical conditions or disorders in the disease management program. They are:

1. Chronicity of the disease
2. Expensive and high prevalence rate of the disease
3. High rate of variability in physician-to-physician treatment patterns
4. Disease episodes can be easily identifiable
5. High rate of patient noncompliance with treatment

From the above criteria, the following medical conditions have been included in the disease management programs. These are:

1. AIDS
2. Asthma
3. Chronic Obstructive Pulmonary Disease (COPD)

4. Congestive Heart Failure (CHF)
5. Cancer
6. Depression
7. Diabetes
8. End-stage Renal Disease

Disease Management Process

In order to successfully execute the disease management programs, each component of the program should be properly utilized throughout the disease management process. Health plans must immediately determine what deficiencies in current disease treatment exist, and what achievable and measurable outcomes should be the objectives for disease management initiatives. There are four important components of disease management programs. These are:

1. Program must have a proper way to address disease prevention
2. Program must provide in-depth education to providers and patients
3. Program must provide timely and accurate diagnosis
4. Program must include treatment protocols to treat exacerbation and complication associated with disease

Currently, disease management programs have had the greatest success with asthma, congestive heart failure, and AIDS.

26. Collaborative Practice Agreements

Collaborative practice agreements (CPAs) refer to the practice where prescribers (generally physicians) authorize pharmacists to engage in specified activities, such as adjusting and/or initiating drug therapy, to help patients achieve more effective and efficient drug therapy outcomes.

CPAs, which must be between a licensed practitioner and a licensed pharmacist, may include:

1. Initiating,
2. Modifying, and administering drug therapy;
3. Ordering and evaluating lab work;
4. Making physical assessments; and providing drug therapy and
5. Patient care management within the scope of practice and practice skills of the parties involved.

The CPAs documents often authorize activity for the specific duration (usually not exceeding two years).

Examples of where CPAs are being used successfully include immunizations, emergency contraception, asthma therapy management, dyslipidemia therapy management, warfarin anticoagulant therapy management, diabetes therapy management, smoking cessation therapy, and flu/antiviral therapy.

Currently, 45 states allow CPAs. Others are developing or reviewing proposed legislation or regulations that would enable pharmacists to participate in CPAs. Most of the earlier CPA initiatives were more commonly implemented in hospital or health-system pharmacy practices, where the oversight of the pharmacy and therapeutics committee made such arrangements more desirable.

However, many states now authorize CPAs to be utilized in additional pharmacy practice settings outside of the hospital, allowing pharmacists to play an increasingly important role in patient care. The types of disease that are most frequently managed by pharmacists in collaboration with physicians are diabetes, asthma, hyperlipidemia, and blood disorder.

The therapies listed as being most frequently the subject of CPAs between pharmacists and physicians are those that can be monitored by the pharmacist through the test of drug efficacy (ie, blood glucose for diabetes, peak flow meter for asthma, blood lipids for hyperlipidemia, and the INR [international normalized ratio] for anticoagulation therapy).

CPAs allowing pharmacists to administer immunizations, especially in the community setting, are becoming an increasing opportunity for pharmacists across the country. Currently, every state has laws or regulations in place allowing pharmacists to administer immunizations. Pharmacists interested in this type of practice should contact their state board of pharmacy and state and national pharmacy associations to learn the specifics of how this particular value-added service can be incorporated into their practice setting.

Components of collaborative practice agreements (CPAs):

Traditional CPAs generally include a number of components. A common component is that one or more pharmacists voluntarily agree to work with one or more prescribers under a written and signed agreement to perform certain patient care functions under specified conditions. Furthermore, most CPAs require the patient or patient's authorized representative to grant his or her informed consent to the collaborative practice.

Common goals for collaborative practice agreements (CPAs):

1. To promote the most efficient and clinically appropriate use of resources
2. To collect valuable outcomes and/or utilization data
3. To communicate to referring physicians the patient outcomes those have resulted from pharmacy care interventions
4. To increase satisfaction for patients, families, staff, physicians, and third-party payers
5. To achieve continuous quality improvement in patient lives and outcomes
6. To serve as a marketing tool to attract patients, staff, or managed-care organizations

Common barriers for collaborative pharmacy practice:

1. Communication breakdowns
2. Lack of trust in another practitioner's competence
3. Practice sites distant from one another
4. Time limitations
5. Confusion or resistance by patients
6. Unclear roles and expectations
7. Reimbursement constraints
8. Lack of prescriptive authority
9. Economic issues

Requirements (pharmacists) for collaborative pharmacy practice:

1. Commission for Certification in Geriatric Pharmacy board certification (CGP)
2. Board of Pharmaceutical Specialties certification
3. American Society of Health-System Pharmacist accredited residency
4. Other clinical residency
5. Completion of a continuing education certificate program in at least one chronic disease state
6. PharmD degree
7. Master's degree
8. Specific number of years of clinical experience
9. Board of Pharmacy approved education/training
10. Specified annual continuing education.

Financial Management of Pharmacies

27. Financial Management of Pharmacies

Functions of Ratios In Financial Analysis: There are a few important ratios that indicate the profitability, efficiency and overall financial positions of a pharmacy.

A. **Ratios Indicating Profitability:**

1. Net Profit To Net Sales (NP:NS)
2. Net Profit To Net Worth (NP:NW)
3. Net Profit To Total Assets (NP:TA)
4. Net Profit To Inventory (NP:IN)

1. **Net Profit To Net Sales (NP:NS):** It can be calculated by dividing net profit by net sales. It is expressed as a percentage. The normal ratio lies between 3 and 7%.

2. **Net Profit To Net Worth (NP:NW):** It can be calculated by dividing net profit by net worth. It is considered the best among other ratios for calculating profitability. The ratio lies between 20 and 25%. 15% is acceptable for older pharmacies and 40% is attainable for newer pharmacies.

3. **Net Profit To Total Assets (NP:TA):** It is normally calculated by dividing net profit by total assets. The normal acceptable ratio lies between 10 and 15%.

4. **Net Profit To Inventory (NP:IN):** It can be calculated by dividing net profit by inventories. It is a good indicator of both profitability and efficiency. The normal acceptable ratio lies between $0.21 and $0.27.

B. **Ratio Indicating Efficiency:**

1. Inventory Turnover Rate (IN:TOR)
2. Net Sales To Inventory (NS:IN)
3. Net Sales To Net Working Capital (NS:NWC)
4. Net Sales To Net Worth (NS:NW)
5. Account Receivable Collection Time (A/R CT)
6. Accounts Payable Remittance Type (A/P RT)

1. **Inventory Turnover Rate:** It is normally calculated by dividing the cost of goods sold by the average of beginning and ending inventory. The inventory turnover rate should be 4 as a minimum, with a target of 6 or higher.

2. **Net Sales To Inventory:** It can be calculated by dividing net sales by net inventory. The ratio normally ranges between 6 and 9.

3. **Net Sales To Net Working Capital:** The net working capital turnover is computed by dividing net sales by net working capital. Networking capital assets is current assets minus current liabilities. The normal ratio range is between 4 and 8. Ratios greater than 8 are considered inadequate capitalization or overtrading. A value below 4 indicates under trading or too much capitalization.

4. **Net Sales To Net Worth:** This is normally calculated by dividing net sales by net worth. Net worth is normally expressed by total assets minus total liabilities. The normal ratio range is between 3 and 8. Greater than 8 is considered under-capitalization and overtrading while below 3 indicates under trading.

5. **Accounts Receivable Collection Time (A/R):** It is normally calculated by dividing an average account receivable by mean credit sales per day. This ratio is a direct measure of the efficient credit management. Normally, a 30-day collection period is the reasonable target.

$$\text{Account Receivable Collection Time} = \frac{\text{Average account receivable}}{\text{Annual Sales } \div 365}$$

6. **Accounts Payable Remittance Time (A/P):** This is normally calculated by an average account payable divided by mean credit purchase per day.

$$\text{Account Payable Remittance Time} = \frac{\text{Average account payable}}{\text{Annual Purchases } \div 365}$$

Liquidity normally measures the pharmacy's ability to meet its current liabilities with little or no interruption in the regular conduct of business.

Solvency measures a pharmacy's ability to meet current liabilities with a moderate change in the composition of current assets.

C. Ratio Indicating Liquidity And Solvency:

1. Acid Test Ratio
2. Current Ratio
3. Inventory To Net Working Capital (IN:NWC)

1. **Acid Test Ratio**: It is also known as quick ratio. It is normally calculated by dividing the sum of cash and accounts receivable by the current liabilities. The normal ratio is 1:1.

2. **Current Ratio**: It is calculated by dividing current assets by current liabilities. The minimum standard value is 2:1.

3. **Inventory To Net Working Capital**: It is calculated by dividing mean inventory by NWC. Mean inventory is the average of the beginning and ending inventory for the accounting period. This ratio is an indirect measure of liquidity and solvency.

   The higher ratio indicates low liquidity and excessive inventory. A ratio of 80% is the reasonable target.

D. Ratio Indicating Financial Position:

1. Total Liabilities To Net Worth (TL:NW)
2. Founded Debt To Net Working Capital (FD:NWC)
3. Fixed Assets To Net Worth (FA:NW)

1. **Total Liabilities To Net Worth:** This ratio can be calculated by dividing total liabilities by net worth. It is expressed as a percentage. It is the most direct measure of the financial position of the pharmacy. A ratio of 50% or lower is acceptable.

2. **Founded Debt To Net Working Capital:** It is normally calculated by dividing long term liabilities by net working capital. It is also expressed as a percentage. Long term liabilities are defined as liabilities extending longer than one year. The normal acceptable value of ratio is between 20 and 25.

3. **Fixed Assets To Net Worth:** This is calculated by dividing depreciated fixed assets by net worth. It helps identifying overinvestment in fixed assets. A higher value indicates over investment in fixed assets while the lower value indicates the need for remodeling. The target value should be 20% or less.

Financial Statement Analysis in the U.S. Healthcare System

There are three approaches normally used to analyze financial statements:

1. Horizontal Analysis
2. Vertical Analysis
3. Ratio Analysis

1. **Horizontal Analysis:** In this type of analysis, the percentage change in a line item from one year to the next is calculated and expressed as the percentage change.

For example, RXCare Pharmacy has the following operating income for year 2013 to 2017:

	2013	**2014**	**2015**	**2016**	**2017**
Operating Income In Millions	1.5	1.1	4.2	6.7	8.2
% Change From Previous Year	0	-26.66%	281.81%	59.52%	22.38%

To find out the Horizontal Analysis 2013-2014:

$$\% \text{ Change} = \frac{\text{Subsequent Year} - \text{Previous Year}}{\text{Previous Year}} \text{ x } 100$$

$$\% \text{ Change} = \frac{1.1 - 1.5}{1.5} \text{ x } 100 = -26.66\%$$

Horizontal Analysis by using year 2016-2017 operating income would be:

$$\% \text{ Change} = \frac{\text{Subsequent Year} - \text{Previous Year}}{\text{Previous Year}} \text{ x } 100$$

$$\% \text{ Change} = \frac{8.2 - 6.7}{6.7} \text{ x } 100 = 22.38\%$$

Disadvantages:

1. Since the Horizontal analysis completely relies on operating income changes, it is hard to determine other factors that may affect these changes. Consider another example, let's say the RXCare Pharmacy operating income for the fiscal year 2016 is $1800,000 and for 2017 is $2550,000. According to Horizontal analysis, RXCare Pharmacy percent in operating-income change would be:

$$\% \text{ Change} = \frac{\text{Subsequent Year} - \text{Previous Year}}{\text{Previous Year}} \text{ x } 100$$

$$\% \text{ Change} = \frac{2550{,}000 - 1800{,}000}{1800{,}000} \text{ x } 100 = 41.66\%$$

This shows 41.66% increased in operating income, however if we look closely the balance sheet,

	2016	**2017**
Operating Revenue	1800,000	2550,000
Interest	300,000 (16.66%)	50,000 (1.96%)
Net Income	1500,000	2500,000

For 2016, the rate of interest is 16.66% on total operating income while, for fiscal year 2017, the rate of interest is only 1.96% and which is a major contributing factor for increasing net operating income of the RXCare Pharmacy. This type of information cannot be analyzed by studying Horizontal analysis.

2. **Trend Analysis:** This is similar to the Horizontal analysis. The only difference is that instead of looking at the single year change, it compares changes over a longer period of time by comparing each year to the base year.

So by using the Trend Analysis, the percent change from 2013 to 2016 would be:

$$\% \text{ Change} = \frac{\text{Subsequent Year} - \text{Previous Year}}{\text{Previous Year}} \text{ x } 100$$

$$\% \text{ Change} = \frac{6.7-1.5}{1.5} \text{ x } 100 = 346.66\%$$

Thus from 2013 to 2016, the operating income of RX Care Pharmacy rose 346.66%. The average annual increase would be 86.6% (346.66/4). An average annual increase in Trend Analysis is different from an individual year percent change found in the Horizontal Analysis.

3. **Vertical Analysis:** The Vertical analysis compares the one line item of the base year to another line item of the subsequent year. It is also known as a common size analysis since it converts every line item to percentages and thus allows comparisons among the financial statement of different companies. Since all final figures are expressed as a percentage, we can also compare different organizations by using the Vertical Analysis. For example, from the list of ten organizations, we can find out which organization has the highest figure in the form of the percentages.

RX Care Pharmacy

	2016	% of Total Revenue	2017	% of Total Revenue
Total Operating Revenue	$2000,000	100%	$1700,000	100%
Total Operating Expenses	$700,000	35%	$250,000	14.7%
Operating Income	$500,000	25%	$500,000	29.41%
Non-Operating Revenue	$200,000	10%	$200,000	11.76%

The Vertical Analysis can be conducted by using the following formula:

$$\text{Vertical Analysis} = \frac{\text{Line Item of Interest}}{\text{Base Line Item}} \text{ x } 100$$

If you carefully look at the chart, you will notice that from 2016 to 2017, there is a decrease in operating revenue (2 million to 1.7 million). However, the net operating income has increased from 25% to 29.41%. This is the advantage of Vertical analysis over the Horizontal analysis. The same figure would have shown the negative percent change in the Horizontal analysis.

$$\% \text{ Change} = \frac{\text{Subsequent Year} - \text{Previous Year}}{\text{Previous Year}} \text{ x } 100$$

$$\% \text{ Change} = \frac{1700{,}000 - 2000{,}000}{1700{,}000} \text{ x } 100 = -15\%$$

This gives the first impression that RX Care Pharmacy is losing money in the business, but when we conduct the Vertical analysis using the same figures, we can be sure that even though operating revenue has declined for the fiscal year 2017, there is no need to worry, since the net operating income for the same fiscal year has increased over 4.41% (29.41% - 25%).

28. Financial Statements and Relative Terms

There are two financial statements normally used by pharmacies. These include:

1. Income Statement
2. Balance Sheet

1. **Income Statement:** It is often known as a profit or loss statement. It shows us the net income of business for a specific period of time. It can be calculated by using the following formula:

Net Income = Total Revenues - Total Expenses

A. **Revenues:** They are defined as cash or promises of cash that flow into the business as a result of business operations. The sale of prescription and OTC drugs, medical equipments and accessories, and health and beauty aids can be considered as the revenue of the pharmacy. However, the sale part of other commodities or services which is not directly affiliated with the owner's primary business cannot be considered as revenue of the pharmacy. For example, revenue obtained from selling the delivery car of pharmacy since selling the car is not the part of pharmacy business; this cannot be included in revenue section of the pharmacy.

B. **Expenses:** They are defined as all costs that are incurred during the operation of the pharmacy. Most of these expenses are incurred to sell products or earn revenue.

C. **Net Income:** It can be defined as the difference between total revenue to the total expenses of the pharmacy for a specific period of time.

2. **Balance Sheet:** It is a financial statement that indicates the current financial status of pharmacy.

Balance sheet has three major components:

A. Assets
B. Liability
C. Owner's equity

A. **Assets:** They are defined as valuable resources which are owned by the business. They can be subdivided into two categories:

A. Current Assets
B. Non-Current Assets

a. **Current Assets:** They are defined as assets which can be easily converted into cash. For example, cash, accounts receivable, inventory etc. When listed on the balance sheet, the current asset which can be easily converted to cash should appear first, followed by other current assets. For example, accounts receivable, cash, and inventory can be listed as:

Current Assets:

1. Cash
2. Accounts receivable (easy to convert into cash compared to an inventory)
3. Inventory

Accounts Receivable: It is defined as money that is going to be received from customers as a result of ordinary extension of credit.

Short-term Investment or Temporary Investment:

At a certain period of the year, a pharmacy may have more cash than is required to operate the business. At that time, instead of leaving cash in a checking account, the pharmacy may invest such money into certificates of deposits, stocks, mutual funds, or bonds in order to obtain the higher rate of return. When these stocks, bonds or mutual funds are sold by companies during the current operating cycle of business, the investments are called short-term investments or temporary investments.

Prepaid Expenses: It is defined as an expense that needs to be paid in advance in order to obtain goods or services. For example, many pharmacies may be required to pay in advance for leasing or renting the business place.

Noncurrent Assets: It is also known as a fixed asset. These assets cannot be sold, consumed or converted to cash within the current operating cycle of business (usually one year). Examples of noncurrent assets are:

1. Land
2. Buildings
3. Fixtures
4. Cars
5. Computers

B. **Liabilities:** In simple terms, liabilities are business debts. Purchasing goods or services on credit, or borrowing money from banks or other financial institutions to finance the business, may create liabilities. Like assets, they can be subdivided into the following categories:

1. Current Liabilities
2. Non-Current Liabilities

1. **Current Liabilities:** They normally arise from debts that will come due during the current operating cycle. The following are examples of current liabilities:

A. Accounts Payable
B. Short-Term Notes Payable
C. Accrued Expenses
D. Current Portion of Long-Term Debt

a. **Accounts Payable:** It is defined as debts that arise from purchasing goods or services on credit.

b. **Short-Term Notes Payable:** It is defined as debt that arises when the pharmacy borrows money from a bank or any other financial institution with a written agreement that specifies when repayment must be made and at what rate of interest.

c. **Accrued Expenses:** These are amounts owed by a pharmacy for purchasing goods or services for which payments have not been made. For example, at the end of the accounting period, the pharmacy may owe its employees for salaries that will not be paid until sometimes in the next accounting period. This may occur when the end of the accounting period falls in the middle of a 2-week period.

d. **Current Portion of Long-Term Debts:** Many times some portion of long-term debts (e.g. car loan, pharmacy mortgage) may be due in a current operating cycle of business, and therefore it is defined under current portion of long-term debts. For example, the amount of the pharmacy's mortgage that must be paid in the current accounting period should be listed under current liabilities. The amount due in the later period should be listed under noncurrent liabilities.

2. **Noncurrent Liabilities:** These are debts that will come due after the current operating cycle of business. For example, a pharmacy mortgage that should be paid off over 20 years.

C **Owner's Equity:** It is a difference between pharmacy's total liabilities (total debts) to its total assets (total equity). It is also known as net worth, stockholders' equity or capital. It arises from two main sources:

1. Invested Capitals
2. Retained Earning

1. **Invested Capital:** It consists of cash invested into the business by its owners. Therefore, the transfer of cash from the owner's personal account to the business account is considered an investment in the business. The opposite is also true; an owner can also withdraw cash from the business. For a corporation, they are called dividends paid. Dividends paid or cash withdrawal may reduce the owner's equity.

2. **Retained Earnings:** These are profits or losses that are incurred during business's current operating cycles. Profits may increase retained earning while losses may reduce them.

29. Depreciation

To operate the pharmacy business, an owner must acquire land, a building, fixtures, computers, delivery cars, etc. These are called noncurrent assets. Pharmacies purchase these noncurrent assets in order to generate revenue and to run a business.

Since the business is using these assets in order to generate income or revenue, costs related to each item must be taken as expenses when preparing financial statements. However, these noncurrent assets are used to generate revenue over several years, and therefore their total costs cannot be recognized as an expense in the year during which they were purchased. Rather, part of their total costs must be counted as an expense in each of the years of their useful life. These costs can be calculated by finding out depreciation values of noncurrent assets.

Depreciation: It is the process of systematically or rationally determining how much the noncurrent asset's initial cost is recognized as an expense in each year of its useful life. Land is an exception, it cannot be depreciated.

Different Methods To Calculate Depreciation Values

To calculate annual depreciation costs of noncurrent assets, we must know values of asset's acquisition costs, asset's useful lives, and asset's estimated residual or salvage values.

1. **Asset's Acquisition Cost:** It is the amount that is paid by the pharmacy for the asset. These costs may include transportation, taxes, and set-up costs that may be incurred during the process of setting up assets in order to run the business. In addition to this, any cost that may be incurred for renovating or overhauling assets should be also included in the acquisition costs. For example, if the pharmacy purchased the building and had it renovated, then the price paid to purchase the building and to renovate it must be included in the acquisition costs.

2. **Asset's Useful Life:** The next step is required to calculate an asset's useful life. It is normally a period of time for which the pharmacy intends to hold the asset. For example, the pharmacy may calculate the useful life for a building at 20 years.

3. **Asset's Estimated Residual or Salvage Value:** The final step would be finding an asset's worth at the end of its useful life. To calculate the asset's worth, the pharmacy must consider what would be the selling price of the assets at the end of its useful life.

Methods For Calculating Depreciations

There are three principal methods to calculate an annual depreciation expense. These are:

1. Straight Line Method
2. Sum Of Years Digits
3. Double Declining Balance Method

1. **Straight Line Method**: This method assumes that noncurrent assets wear out at a constant rate and as a result the annual depreciation expense is the same in each year of the asset's life. It can be calculated by using the following formula:

$D = (C - R) \times \frac{1}{N}$

D = Depreciation expenses
C = Cost
R = Residual value
N = Number of years of useful life of assets

Example: What would be the depreciation expense of noncurrent assets having (C-R) = \$15,000 and a predicted useful life of asset is 10 years.

$$D = (C - R) \times \frac{1}{N}$$
$$D = (15000) \times \frac{1}{10}$$
$$D = \$1500 \text{ each year for 10 years}$$

2. **Sum of Years Digits:** This is defined under accelerated methods of calculating depreciation expenses. It is based on the assumption that the asset loses more of its value in the early years of its life. For example, a car (noncurrent asset) loses much more of its value in the first year after its purchase than in later years. This method calculates depreciation expenses by the sum of years digits method. It can be calculated by using the following formula:

$$D = (C - R) \times \frac{I}{N}$$

D = Depreciation expenses
C = Cost
R = Residual value
N = Number of years of useful life of assets
I = Sum of years digits

Example: What would be the depreciation expenses of a noncurrent asset in its third year of predicted useful life? The number of useful life of noncurrent asset is 5 years, and (C-R = \$40,000).

	Year	C – R	N/I	D
	1	40,000	5/15	13333
	2	40,000	4/15	10666
	3	40,000	3/15	8000
	4	40,000	2/15	5333
	5	40,000	1/15	2660
Sum of Years (I)	**15**			

Therefore, the predicted depreciation expenses of a noncurrent asset in its third year of useful life would be \$8000 (40,000 x 3/15 = 8000).

3. **Double Declining Balance Method:** The annual depreciation expense under this method can be calculated by multiplying the book value of the asset by twice the straight line rate of depreciations. The book value of asset can be calculated by subtracting the asset's accumulated depreciation from its original acquisition cost.

Book Value = Actual Cost - Accumulated Depreciation Cost

Straight Line Method

Year	C - R	r (Straight Line Rate)	Depreciation
1	30,000	1/5	6000
2	30,000	1/5	6000
3	30,000	1/5	6000
4	30,000	1/5	6000
5	30,000	1/5	6000

Example: What would be the 4th year accumulated depreciation for the asset with an acquisition cost of $30000? Assume that the product useful life is 5 years. By using double declining balance method:

Double Declining Balance Method

Year	Book Value	Double Straight Line Rate	Depreciation	Accumulated Depreciation
1	30000	2/5	12000	12000
2	18000	2/5	7200	19200
3	10800	2/5	4320	23520
4	6480	2/5	2592	26112
5	3888	2/5	1555.20	27667.20

The acquisition cost of asset is $30000. The amount is multiplied by double the straight line rate (straight line rate for each year for 5 years useful life of the asset will be 1/5 and multiplied it by two gives 2/5) that gives us the first year depreciation cost of $12000. When calculating for second year, the book value of the asset is going to be acquisition minus accumulated depreciation cost, and therefore second year depreciation cost would be:

= 18000 x 2/5 (Book value = 30000 – 12000 = 18000)
= 7200

Similarly, we can find the 4th year accumulated depreciation cost for the asset; it would be $26112.

The process is continued for each year. However, one has to make sure that any time during the useful life period of an asset, the accumulated depreciation cannot exceed the principal acquisition cost of the asset or in other words we can say that the maximum accumulated depreciation cost should be equal or less than the acquisition cost of the asset. For example, in above calculation, the five year depreciation expenses ($27667.20) cannot exceed the original acquisition cost of the asset ($30000).

30. Inventory and Cost of Goods Sold

Inventory is defined as all goods that a pharmacy holds for resale. It is an asset. Cost of goods sold refers to the cost of merchandise that the pharmacy has sold during the year. Cost of goods sold is an expense. Inventory and cost of goods sold may be measured by using either of these two systems:

1. Perpetual System
2. Periodic System

Out of these two, a perpetual system is more useful and logical but requires a great deal of recording:

1. **Perpetual System:** It maintains the current and accurate account for inventory and cost of goods sold. When the pharmacy purchases any merchandise, the balance in the inventory account is increased by the amount of the purchase, and when the pharmacy sells merchandise, the balance in the inventory account is reduced. As a rule of thumb, when the balance in the inventory account is decreased, the balance in the cost of goods sold account is increased by the cost of the item sold.

This system requires separate inventory accounts for each stock keeping unit (SKU). For example, Lanoxin is available in 0.125 and 0.25 mg strengths, and in package sizes 100, 500, and 1000. A pharmacy using the perpetual system requires separate SKUs for each different size and strength of Lanoxin.

For each SKU, the account is supposed to show beginning inventory, and all sales and purchases made throughout the year. Any time during the year the sale or purchase of the particular SKU is made, inventory accounts must be updated. Because of this, the perpetual system provides an accurate and updated report of any merchandise (SKU) during any time of the year.

2. **Periodic System:** This system is simpler than the perpetual inventory system which requires lots of attention and record keeping requirements. However, this system cannot provide you with as accurate and updated inventory record as perpetual inventory system.

This system requires accounts for sales, purchases and inventory in order to find the account balance and costs of goods sold. It does require the inventory balance be updated for each sale or purchase made. Cost of goods sold under this system can be calculated by the following formula:

$$\text{Cost of Goods Sold} = \begin{matrix}\text{Beginning}\\\text{Inventory}\end{matrix} + \begin{matrix}\text{Purchases Made}\\\text{Throughout the}\\\text{Year}\end{matrix} - \begin{matrix}\text{Ending Inventory}\\\text{At the End of the}\\\text{Year}\end{matrix}$$

Inventory Valuation Methods

Inventory Valuation Methods: There are three methods by which a pharmacy can assign a value to each commodity present in the inventory. These are:

1. Weighted Average Cost Method (WAC)
2. First In, First Out Method (FIFO)
3. Last In, First Out Method (LIFO)

Lanoxin Inventory Data As Per Periodic System

	No. of Bottles	Unit Cost($)	Total Cost($)
Beginning Inventory	30	20	600
March Purchases	10	30	300
June Purchases	10	40	400
September Purchases	5	50	250
Total Goods Available for Sale	55		1550
Ending Inventory	10		?
Goods Sold	45		?

1. **Weighted Average Cost Method (WAC):** This method estimates a cost which represents the cost of the product over the entire accounting period. The weighted average cost of each unit is determined and multiplied by the number of total units.

   For example, an inventory data shows 55 bottles of Lanoxin available for sale during the year. The total cost of goods available for sale is $1550, therefore the weighted average cost (WAC) per bottle would be:

$$\text{WAC} = \frac{\text{Total Cost of Goods Available for Sale (COGAS)}}{\text{Number of Bottles Available for Sale}}$$

$$\text{WAC} = \frac{1550}{55} = \$28.18 \text{ per bottle}$$

From table, we can say that 10 bottles were remaining in ending inventory or 45 bottles were sold during the year, therefore:

1. Ending Inventory = 10 bottles x $28.18 = $281.80
2. Cost of Goods Sold = 45 bottles x $28.18 = $1268.18

2. **<u>First In, First Out Method (FIFO):</u>** This method is based on the assumption that the first units bought are the first sold. Referring to table 2.0, this method assumes that 30 bottles of Lanoxin present at the beginning of inventory are sold first, followed by the next 10 purchased in March, then 10 in June, and the last 5 purchased in September.

<u>By using this method, the first 45 bottles cost of goods sold can be calculated as:</u>

= 30 bottles x \$20 per bottle + 10 bottles x \$30 per bottle + 5 bottles x \$40 per bottle
= \$600 + \$300 + \$200
= \$1100

<u>A total of 10 bottles is remaining in ending inventory (EI), therefore:</u>

EI = 5 bottles x \$40 (June purchases) + 5 bottles x \$50 (September purchases)
EI = \$200 + \$250 = \$450

3. **<u>Last In, First Out (LIFO):</u>** This method is also known as LIFO. It is based on assumption that the last product purchased is the first to go and that the first purchase is the last to go.

<u>If we apply this method to the previous example, the cost of goods sold would be:</u>

= 5 bottles x \$50 per bottle + 10 bottles x \$40 per bottle + 10 bottles x \$30 per bottle + 20 bottles x \$20 per bottle

= \$250 + \$400 + \$300 + \$400
= \$1350

This method assumes that 10 bottles in ending inventory are the first 10 purchased, therefore:

Ending Inventory = 10 bottles x \$20 (beginning inventory at price of \$ 20 per bottle)
= \$200

With the help of this method, cost of goods sold can be manipulated by buying extra units of a good at the end of accounting period.

<u>Comparison of LIFO and FIFO</u>

When prices were increasing throughout the year, FIFO gave the lowest cost of goods sold, while LIFO gave the highest. The opposite is also true, if the price of goods is decreasing over a period of time, the FIFO would have given the highest cost of goods sold while LIFO would have yielded the lowest. During recent years costs of pharmaceutical products have increased dramatically. By using the LIFO method, a pharmaceutical company can yield the highest cost of goods sold. Because of this, LIFO would earn the lowest pretax income, and therefore the lowest tax payments. This may increase the financial cash flow as well as its actual income. Therefore it is advisable to use the LIFO method when product's prices are increasing over a period of time.

Estimating Inventory Level by Using Gross Margin Method

Beginning Inventory	$45000
Purchases	$80000
Sales	$100,000
Average Gross Margin Present In Past Years	40%

Every pharmacy normally takes its physical inventory at least once a year. Since taking an inventory is time consuming and very expensive, it is physically and economically not possible for the pharmacy to take the inventory more frequently.

However, a pharmacy may want to find out the financial status of business more often than this. This can be done by estimating the current level of inventory without taking the physical inventory.

To estimate an inventory level by using this method, the pharmacy shall find out the percent of cost of goods sold. It can be calculated by using the following formula:

% cost of goods sold = 1 - % gross margin
% cost of goods sold = 1 - 40% (from table)
% cost of goods sold = 60% or 0.6

From the above value, we can find out the dollar amount of cost of goods sold:

Cost of goods sold = sales x % cost of goods sold
Cost of goods sold = $100000 x 0.6
Cost of goods sold = $60000

When these values are inserted in the following equation, it gives us the value of ending inventory:

Cost of Goods Sold = Beginning Inventory + Purchases - Ending Inventory

60,000 = 45,000 + 80,000 - Ending Inventory, therefore

Ending Inventory = $65,000

With the help of cost of goods sold and ending inventory values, the pharmacy can generate the current financial status of the pharmacy.

31. Break Even Analysis (BEA)

Break Even Analysis: It is a technique by which pharmacy managers can make a decision by predicting the effects of changes in costs, prices, or revenues on pharmacy profits. At the Break Even Point (BEP), the total sales of the pharmacy equal total costs.

There are three types of costs that affect overall pharmacy expenses. These are:

1. Fixed costs
2. Variable costs
3. Semi-variable costs

1. Fixed Costs: This type of cost remains the same regardless of profit or loss in the business. Examples of fixed costs are:

1. Depreciation Costs
2. Business Property Tax
3. Business License Fees

2. Variable Costs: They are defined as costs that are directly proportional to sale volume of the business. Examples of variable costs are:

1. The costs of goods sold. As sales increase, the cost of goods sold will also increase.

2. Costs to purchase supplies and accessories. As sales increase, more prescription bottles, prescription labels and ink cartridge are required.

3. Any commission or franchise fees. As sales increase, more franchise fees must be paid.

3. Semi-Variable Costs: These types of costs include both fixed and variable component of costs. Examples of semi-variable costs are:

1. Rent of pharmacy fees which are based on a fixed monthly fee plus some percentage of sales and utility rates.

BEA can be conducted by using the following methods:

1. Graphically
2. A contribution margin approach

RX Care Pharmacy Financial Data	
Total Sales	$1000,000
Cost of Goods Sold	$600,000
Gross Margin	$400,000
Fixed Expenses	$180,000
Variable Expenses	$620,000
Miscellaneous Expenses	$20,000
Net Income	$200,000

1. **Graphical method to calculate the Break Even Point:**

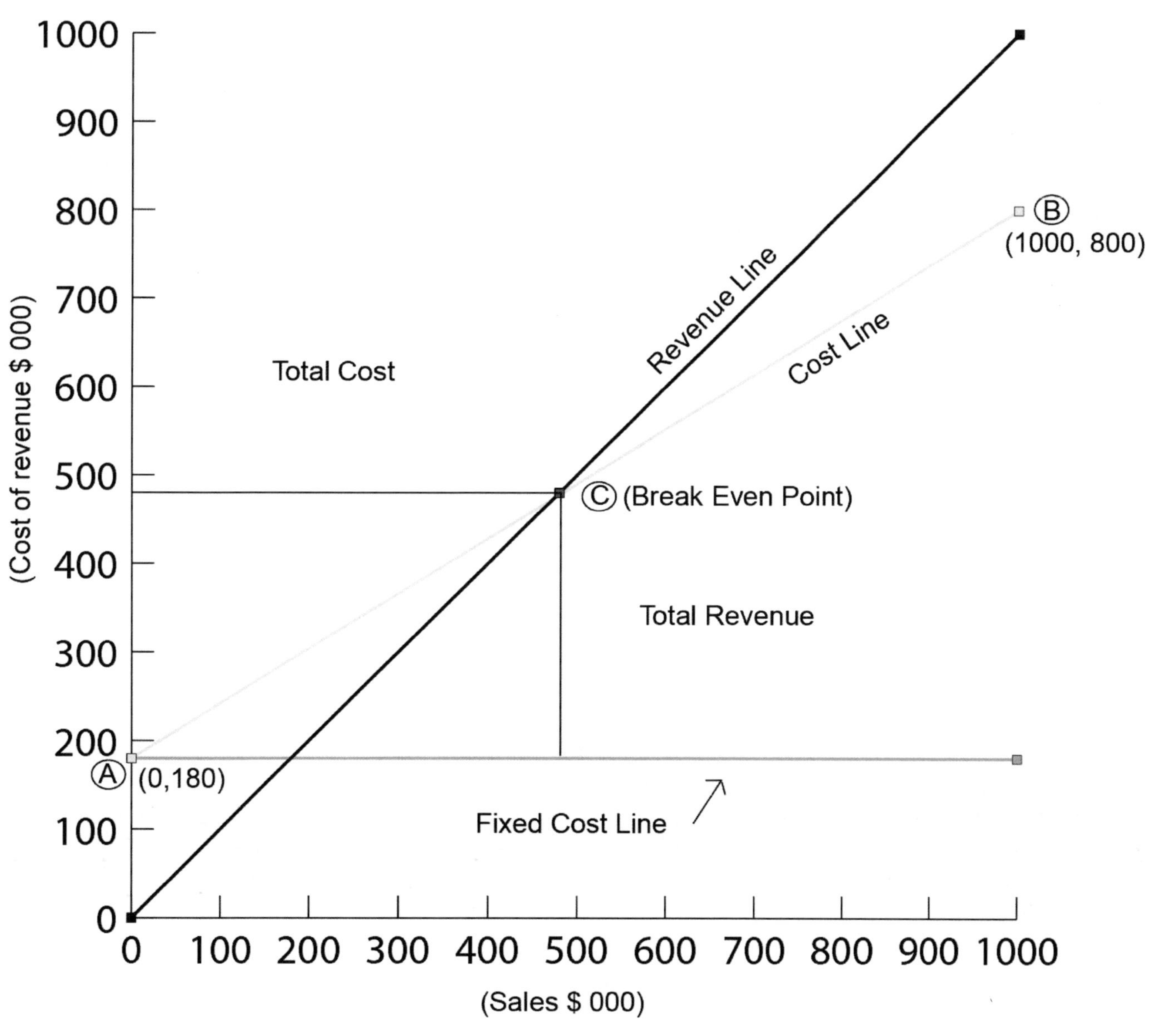

A. **Total Revenue Line:** It is defined as a line beginning at the origin (0,0) and having a slope of 1 (see figure). Total revenue line always has the slope of 1.

B. **Fixed Costs Line:** When a pharmacy has zero sales, its total costs would be equal to its fixed costs. For RX Care Pharmacy, this would be point A (0,180) in figure.

C. **Total Costs Line:** From the given financial data, we can also find out point B on the graph. For example, when RX Care Pharmacy's total sale volume is $1000,000; its total costs (fixed expenses + variable expenses = {costs of goods sold + miscellaneous expenses}) would be $800,000. This will give us a point B (1000, 800). Join point A and point B with a straight line. This is going to be our total costs line.

D. **Break Even Point:** The point at which the total revenue line intersects the total cost line is defined as the Break Even Point. In a given graph, this point is designated as point C (473.68, 473.68). This indicates that RX Care Pharmacy will make a profit when its sale volume exceeds $473,000, and at a sale volume less than 473,684, the pharmacy will lose money.

2. Contribution Margin Approach To Calculate The Break Even Point

Under this method, the Break Even Point of business can be calculated with the help of the pharmacy's contribution margin.

Contribution Margin (CM) = Total Revenue - Variable Cost (Expenses)

Contribution Margin (CM) = $1000,000 - $620,000
= $ 380,000

Net Income = Contribution Margin - Fixed Costs (expenses)
= $380,000 - $180,000
= $200,000

The contribution margin as the percent of sale can be calculated by using the following formula:

$$\text{CM\%} = \frac{\text{CM}}{\text{Total Sales}} \text{ x } 100$$

$$\text{CM\%} = \frac{380000}{1000{,}000} \text{ x } 100 = 38\%$$

A contribution margin is supposed to be large enough to cover fixed costs. (Net Profit = Contribution Margin - Fixed Costs)

For RX Care Pharmacy, the contribution margin % is 38. Therefore, we can say that for every dollar of sales of RX Care Pharmacy, 38 cents are required to cover the pharmacy's net profit and fixed costs. The other 62 cents (62%) cover the variable costs of RX Care Pharmacy. Therefore, RX Care Pharmacy shall earn at least 38 cents per dollar to cover its fixed costs in order to break even.

To cover $0.38 fixed cost ⟶ Requires $1 sale volume
To cover $180,000 fixed cost ⟶ ?

$$= \frac{180,000 \text{ x } 1}{0.38} = \$473684$$

This is going to be the BEP for RX Care Pharmacy since at this sale volume; the pharmacy will earn enough to cover its fixed costs. For sales revenue greater than $473684, the pharmacy will make a profit of 38 cents per dollar. The other 62 cents will be used to cover variable costs due to an increased sales volume.

Stay Even Point (SEP)

When pharmacy managers make any changes to their pharmacy (i.e. increasing advertising, offering discount), they always look forward to maintaining the pharmacy's current profitability rather than just the break even. The predictable point at which the pharmacy maintains its current profitability even after adding services to the pharmacy is defined as the SEP or Stay Even Point.

The SEP can be calculated by treating net income as an additional fixed cost. For example, RX Care Pharmacy has a net income of $200,000 with fixed costs of $180,000, therefore:

$$\text{SEP} = \frac{(\text{Fixed Cost} + \text{Net Profit})}{\text{CM \%}}$$

$$\text{SEP} = \frac{(180,000 + 200,000)}{0.38} = \$1000,000$$

OR

To cover $0.38 fixed cost ⟶ Requires $1 sale volume
To cover ($180,000 + $200,000) ⟶ ?

$$= \frac{380,000}{0.38} = \$1000,000$$

By treating the net income as an additional cost, RX Care Pharmacy must earn a total sales volume of $1000,000 in order to stay above the BEP.

Example: If RX Care Pharmacy wants to raise its advertisement costs from $5000 to $15,000 per year, what would be Stay Even Point for the pharmacy in order to maintain profitability? [Fixed Cost: $180,000, Net income: $200,000 and CM%: 38%]

An increase in advertisement cost would be $10,000 ($15000 - $5000). Therefore,

$$\text{SEP} = \frac{(\text{Fixed Cost} + \text{Net Profit})}{\text{CM \%}}$$

$$\text{SEP} = \frac{(180,000 + 10,000 \text{ (Advertisement Cost)} + 200,000)}{0.38}$$

A new SEP would be **$1026315.78**

Thus, if RX Care Pharmacy wants to increase its advertising budget by $10,000 per year ($15000 - $5000), the pharmacy must earn the total sales volume of $1026315.78 in order to maintain its profitability level.

32. Types of Costs And Methods for Calculating Product Price

There are mainly two types of costs associated with any pharmacy business. These are:

1. Direct Costs
2. Indirect Costs

1. **Direct Costs:** These costs are directly affiliated with services provided by a pharmacy. Examples of such costs are:

1. Prescription containers
2. Prescription labels
3. Pharmacists' time to provide counseling
4. Pharmacy license fees
5. Continuing education programs costs
6. Patients' education material print out costs
7. Computers and software costs
8. Professional liability insurance

All the above costs are directly affiliated with pharmacy services. For example, if the pharmacy does not dispense a prescription, then costs related to the prescription containers or labels would not occur.

2. **Indirect Costs:** These costs are not directly associated with services provided by the pharmacy. For example, costs related to the store manager's salary, rents and utility expenses of a building would still occur even if the pharmacy does not provide prescription services. These types of costs are classified as indirect expenses. Example: By using the following data, calculate an approximate dispensing cost for RX Care Pharmacy.

Pharmacist's Salary	$90,000
Equipments, prescriptions and containers costs	$20,000
Building rent, utilities and maintenance costs (RX department only)	$10,000
Building rent, utilities and maintenance costs (store)	$40,000
Other indirect costs	$60,000
No of RX dispensed by pharmacy in coming year	40,000

The Cost To Dispense (CTD) can be calculated by using the following formula:

$$\text{CTD} = \frac{(\text{Total Direct Costs} + \text{Total Indirect Costs})}{\text{No. of Prescriptions Dispensed by Pharmacy}}$$

$$\text{CTD} = \frac{(90{,}000\ + 20{,}000) + (10{,}000 + 60{,}000)}{40{,}000}$$

$$\text{CTD} = \frac{(110{,}000) + (70{,}000)}{40{,}000} = \$4.50 \text{ Per Prescription}$$

Based on the data given, RX Care Pharmacy should keep its cost of dispensing to $4.50 per prescription in order to cover its major expenses. If you notice, we have not considered indirect costs of $40,000 in our calculation. Since this figure relates to indirect expenses of the whole store, we cannot include it to count cost toward dispensing prescription.

Methods For Calculating The Product Price

There are three principal methods by which the product price can be calculated. These are:

1. Mark-Up Method
2. Professional Fee Method
3. Sliding Scale Method

1. **Mark-Up Method**: This method relies on the cost of ingredients. The dispensing fees can be calculated by using the following formula:

$$\text{Dispensing Price} = \text{Ingredient Costs} + (\text{Ingredient Costs x \% Mark} - \text{Up})$$

Example: What would be the prescription cost for dispensing 30 tablets of Ketoconazole ($120)? The % mark-up on a prescription is 15.

$$\text{Dispensing Price} = \text{Ingredient Costs} + (\text{Ingredient Costs x \% Mark} - \text{Up})$$

Dispensing Price = 120 + (120 x 0.15)
Dispensing Price = 120 + 18 = $138

The dispensing price for the prescription can also be calculated by using the markup on the retail price method.

Example: If the ingredient costs for 30 tablets of Ketoconazole is $120 and the percentage markup on retail price is 15, what would be the dispensing price of the prescription?

$$\text{Dispensing Price} = \text{Ingredient Costs} + (\text{Price}\ \ \text{x \% Mark} - \text{Up})$$

OR

$$\text{Dispensing Price} = \frac{\text{Ingredient Costs}}{1 - \frac{\text{\% Mark Up}}{100}}$$

$$\text{Dispensing Price} = \frac{120}{1 - \frac{15}{100}}$$

$$\text{Dispensing Price} = \frac{120}{0.85} = \$141.17$$

The markup on retail price method is the most widely used method for determining the dispensing price. Since it determines the price on the basis of markup on retail, one can easily calculate the gross margin on the prescription.

Advantages of Markup Methods:

1. The principal advantage of the markup method is that it protects the pharmacy against the price inflation. As the ingredient cost increases, the dollar margin on the prescription also increases proportionately.

Disadvantages of Markup Methods:

1. The principal disadvantage of the % markup method is that it subsidizes low-cost products with high-cost products. For example, if the pharmacy sells analgesic balm for $6.00 ($5 ingredient cost + 20% mark-up), the pharmacy will make a dollar margin on the prescription which is far lower than the average dispensing cost ($5.00) of the prescription.

   Now consider that the pharmacy is selling Xalatan eye drops, and the dispensing price will be $120 ($100 ingredient cost + 20% mark up on prescription). The dollar margin on this prescription is $20 which is far higher than the average dispensing cost ($5.00) of prescription.

   However, the patient will react to this high price of Xalatan eye drops and may go somewhere else to fill the prescription. On the other hand, when the patient is purchasing an inexpensive drug such as analgesic balm, he or she is unlikely to even notice that the prescription price is exceptionally low.

2. **Professional Fee Method:** This method is widely used by most third party prescription programmers to reimburse pharmacies. Under this method, the price of the prescription can be calculated by adding the fixed amount of predetermined fees to the ingredient costs of the medication. For example, if an ingredient cost of analgesic balm is $5 and fixed reimbursement rate for the prescription is $6, the retail price of the prescription would be $11 ($5 + $6).

   As the dispensing fee (professional fee) remains the same regardless of cost of ingredients, the dispensing price for Xalatan eye drops under this method would be $106 ($100 ingredient cost + $6 professional fee).

Disadvantages of Professional Fee Method:

1. It yields low gross margin on expensive products. For example, the percentage gross margin on Xalatan eye drops would be 6%, which is far lower than the average gross margin percentage on prescription (usually 15 to 20%).

2. This system discourages the pharmacy from carrying expensive drugs. Since the margin on expensive drugs is so low, then it could not even cover the cost to keep the expensive products in the inventory.

3. This system encourages overutilization of prescription drugs. For example, the patient will prefer to buy three months' worth of a medication supply by paying a one-time dispensing fee rather than purchasing the month supply of the drug and paying three times for dispensing fees.

3. **Sliding Scale Method:** As discussed earlier, the mark-up method subsidizes low-cost drugs with high-cost ones, and the professional fee method disregards the higher inventory carrying costs associated with more expensive drugs. The sliding scale method overcomes the disadvantages of both systems.

Under this type of reimbursement method, if the pharmacy uses a % mark-up method, it shall use the variable percentage mark-up method which allows the pharmacy to charge a low % mark-up on expensive drugs and a high % mark up on low-cost products. This will eliminate subsidization of low-cost drugs with expensive ones.

If the pharmacy uses the professional fee method, the sliding scale method advises pharmacies to charge lower dispensing fees on expensive drug products and more for low-cost drug products. These way pharmacies may cover inventory carrying costs for expensive products and at the same time may offer reasonable prices to patients on low-cost products.

Pharmacy Administration & Jurisprudence

33. Pharmacy Law

PURE FOOD AND DRUG ACT OF 1906

Congress passed this law in 1906 to protect people from unsanitary and poorly labeled food.

FOOD, DRUG AND COSMETIC ACT OF 1938

This law suggests that no new drug can be marketed until proven safe by the FDA for public use.

DURHAM HUMPHREY AMENDMENT OF 1951

This law is also known as "Prescription Drug Amendment".

It differentiates between prescription and OTC drugs.

It also authorizes oral prescriptions and prescription refills.

It suggests that each drug should be labeled "Caution: Federal law prohibits dispensing without a prescription."

KEFAUVER HARRIS AMENDMENT OF 1962

It is also known as the "Drug Efficacy Amendment".

This law indicates that new approved drugs must be safe as well as effective.

It also establishes Good Manufacturing Practice requirements.

MEDICAL DEVICE AMENDMENT OF 1976

This law passed in 1976, and includes:

The classification of medical devices

Safety and efficacy of medical devices

ORPHAN DRUG ACT OF 1983

This law was passed for orphan drugs (drugs for diseases that affect very few people). Congress passed this act to provide tax relief and other incentives for the pharmaceutical manufacturers to develop and market orphan drugs.

DRUG PRICE COMPETITION AND PATENT TERM RESTORATION ACT OF 1984

This law is also known as Waxman Hatch Amendment. This law was passed to make generic drugs more readily and easily available to the general public. The law also provides more incentive to innovative pharmaceutical companies and encourages them to develop new drugs.

NATIONAL DRUG CODE NUMBER (NDC)

The NDC generally consists of ten to eleven letters.

The first four characters indicate the name of the manufacturer or distributor.
The middle four characters identify the drug name and strength.
The last two characters identify the package.

NATIONAL PROVIDER IDENTIFIER STANDARD (NPI)

The National Provider Identifier (NPI) is the Health Insurance Portability and Accountability Act (HIPAA) Administrative Simplification Standard.

The NPI is a unique identification number for covered health care providers. Covered health care providers and all health plans and health care clearinghouses must use the NPIs in the administrative and financial transactions adopted under HIPAA.

The NPI is a 10-position, intelligence-free numeric identifier (10-digit number). This means that the numbers do not carry other information about healthcare providers, such as the state in which they live or their medical specialty.

The NPI must be used in lieu of legacy provider identifiers in the HIPAA standards transactions.

OVER THE COUNTER DRUG

The FDA classifies OTC drugs into three different categories.

Category I: It includes ingredients generally considered to be safe, effective and not misbranded.

Category II: It includes ingredients that are not considered to be safe or effective, or are misbranded.

Category III: It includes ingredients for which data are insufficient to permit their classification.

PATIENT PACKAGE INSERT

The FDA passed this law in 1970. The law states that a patient must be provided with the supplement drug information, commonly known as Patient Package Insert or PPI, by a pharmacist while dispensing certain drugs.

The list of such drugs are:

1. Isotretinoin
2. Oral contraceptives
3. Isoproterenol
4. Ticlopidine
5. Progesterone
6. Estrogen
7. Intrauterine device

OBRA ACT OF 1990

It is known as the Omnibus Budget Reconciliation Act of 1990. It requires that pharmacists must offer counseling to a patient.

The FDA Employs A Two Letter Coding System For Therapeutic Equivalence Of Different Drugs

AA: Drugs that are available in conventional dosage forms and have no bioequivalence problems.

AT: Topical drugs that meet bioequivalence standards.

AB: Drugs meeting the necessary bioequivalence requirements.

BC: Drugs in extended release dosage form with bioequivalence issues.

BT: Topical drugs with bioequivalence issues.

BX: Drugs for which adequate information is not available to determine their bioequivalence.

POISON PREVENTION ACT

This law was implemented to prevent the death of children from accidental poisoning. This act was passed in 1973. It indicates that all dispensed drugs must be dispensed in a child proof or a child resistant container.

Drugs Exempt From This Law Are:

1. Sublingual dosage form of nitroglycerine
2. Sublingual and chewable form of Isosorbide dinitrate (less than 10 mg)
3. Cholestyramine powder
4. Methylprednisolone tablets (less than 84 mg)
5. Mebendazole tablets (less than 600 mg of drug)
6. Potassium supplements (unit dose form)
7. Erythromycin ethyl succinate (liquid and granules not more than 8 gm of drug)
8. Colestipol in powder form
9. Erythromycin ethylsuccinate (tablets no more than 16 gm of drug)
10. Pancrelipase preparations
11. Prednisone (tablets no more than 105 mg)
12. Oral contraceptives

CONTROLLED SUBSTANCE ACT

CSA = Controlled Substance Act
DEA = Drug Enforcement Administration

The attorney general of United States has authority to place a drug into one of the five categories of schedule controlled drugs.

The controlled drugs can be classified into five different classes according to their potential for abuse. The potency of abuse of controlled drugs should be I > II > III > IV > V. Schedule I shall be considered the highest potential for abuse whereas schedule V drugs shall be considered the lowest potential for abuse.

SCHEDULE II CONTROLLED DRUGS

- Cannot be refilled under any circumstances.
- The partial filling of this class of drugs should be done within 72 hours of its initial filling.
- The DEA 222 order form is required to order this class of drugs.

LIST OF SCHEDULE II CONTROLLED DRUGS:

1. Alfentanil (Alfenta)
2. Amobarbital (Amytal, Tuinal)
3. Amphetamine (Dexedrine, Biphetamine)
4. Lisdexamfetamine (Vyvanse)
5. Coca Leaves
6. Cocaine
7. Codeine
8. Dextropropoxyphene, bulk (non-dosage forms)
9. Dihydrocodeine (Didrate, Parazone)
10. Diphenoxylate

11. Diprenorphine
12. Ecgonine (Cocaine precursor, in Coca leaves)
13. Ethylmorphine (Dionin)
14. Fentanyl (Innovar, Sublimaze, Duragesic)
15. Glutethimide (Doriden, Dorimide)
16. Hydrocodone (dihydrocodeinone)
17. Hydrocodone and isoquinoline alkaloid
18. Hydrocodone combination product (Tussionex, Tussend, Lortab, Vicodin, Hycodan, Anexsia)
19. Hydromorphone (Dilaudid, dihydromorphinone)
20. Levo-Alphacetylmethadol (LAAM, long acting methadone, levomethadyl acetate)
21. Meperidine (Demerol, Mepergan, Pethidine)
22. Methadone (Dolophine, Methadose, Amidone)
23. Methamphetamine (Desoxyn, D-desoxyephedrine, ICE, Crank, Speed)
24. Methylphenidate (Ritalin)
25. Morphine (MS Contin, Roxanol, Duramorph, RMS, MSIR)
26. Opium poppy
27. Opium tincture
28. Opium, granulated
29. Opium, powdered
30. Opium, raw
31. Oxycodone (OxyContin, Percocet, Tylox, Roxicodone, Roxicet)
32. Oxymorphone (Numorphan)
33. Pentobarbital (Nembutal)
34. Poppy Straw Concentrate
35. Remifentanil (Ultiva)
36. Secobarbital (Seconal, Tuinal)
37. Sufentanil (Sufenta)
38. Tapentadol (Nucynta)

SCHEDULE CIII CIV AND CV CONTROLLED DRUGS

- Cannot be refilled more than five times.
- Cannot be filled/refilled for the prescription older than six months.
- Do not require DEA 222 form to order these classes of drugs.

SCHEDULE III CONTROLLED DRUGS:

1. Amobarbital and non-controlled active ingredients
2. Amobarbital suppository dosage form
3. Anabolic steroids
4. Barbituric acid derivative
5. Benzphetamine (Didrex, Inaptly)
6. Buprenorphine (Buprenex, Temgesic)
7. Butabarbital (Butisol, Butibel)
8. Butalbital (Fiorinal, Butalbital with aspirin)
9. Codeine and isoquinoline alkaloid (Codeine with papaverine or noscapine)
10. Codeine combination product (Empirin, Fiorinal, Tylenol, ASA or APAP w/codeine)

11. Dronabinol in sesame oil in soft gelatin capsule (Marinol)
12. Gamma-hydroxybutyric acid
13. Ketamine
14. Lysergic acid
15. Lysergic acid amide
16. Methyltestosterone (Android, Oreton, Testred, Virilon)
17. Nalorphine (Nalline)
18. Nandrolone (Deca-Durabolin, Durabolin, Durabolin-50)
19. Norethandrolone (Nilevar)
20. Opium combination product (Paregoric)
21. Pentobarbital and non-controlled active ingredients
22. Pentobarbital suppository dosage form
23. Phendimetrazine (Bontril)
24. Secobarbital and non-controlled active ingredients
25. Secobarbital suppository dosage form
26. Sodium oxybate (Xyrem)
27. Testosterone (Android-T, Depotest, Delatestryl)
28. Thiopental (Pentothal)

SCHEDULE IV CONTROLLED DRUGS

1. Tramadol (Ultram)
2. Carisoprodol (Soma)
3. Alprazolam (Xanax)
4. Barbital (Barbitone)
5. Butorphanol (Stadol, Stadol NS, Torbugesic, Torbutrol)
6. Chloral hydrate (Noctec)
7. Chlordiazepoxide (Librium, Libritabs, Limbitrol, SK-Lygen)
8. Clonazepam (Klonopin, Clonopin)
9. Clorazepate(Tranxene)
10. Dexfenfluramine (Redux)
11. Diazepam (Valium, Valrelease)
12. Dichloralphenazone (Midrin)
13. Difenoxin 1 mg/ Atropine 25 mcg (Motofen)
14. Estazolam (ProSom, Domnamid, Eurodin, Nuctalon)
15. Ethchlorvynol (Placidyl)
16. Fenfluramine (Pondimin, Ponderal)
17. Flurazepam (Dalmane)
18. Fospropofol (Lusedra)
19. Lorazepam (Ativan)
20. Mazindol (Sanorex, Mazanor)
21. Meprobamate (Miltown, Equanil, Deprol, Equagesic, Meprospan)
22. Midazolam (Versed)
23. Modafinil (Provigil)
24. Oxazepam (Serax, Serenid-D)
25. Pemoline (Cylert)
26. Pentazocine (Talwin, Talwin NX, Talacen, Talwin Compound)
27. Phenobarbital (Luminal, Donnatal, Bellergal-S)

28. Phentermine (Ionamin, Fastin, Adipex-P, Obe-Nix, Zantryl)
29. Prazepam (Centrax)
30. Propofol (Diprivan)
31. Propoxyphene dosage forms with other ingredients
32. Quazepam (Doral, Dormalin)
33. Sibutramine (Meridia)
34. Temazepam (Restoril)
35. Triazolam (Halcion)
36. Zaleplon (Sonata)
37. Zolpidem (Ambien)
38. Zopiclone (Imovane)
39. Eszopiclone (Lunesta)

SCHEDULE V CONTROLLED DRUGS

1. Codeine preparations - Not more than 200 mg per 100 ml or 100 gm (Robitussin AC, Phenergan with Codeine).
2. Difenoxin preparations - Not more than 0.5 mg Difenoxin + 25mcg Atropine sulfate (Motofen).
3. Dihydrocodeine preparations - Not more than 100 mg per 100 ml or 100 gm.
4. Diphenoxylate preparations- Not more than 2.5 mg Diphenoxylate + 25mcg Atropine sulfate (Lomotil, Logen).
5. Ethylmorphine preparations - Not more than 100 mg per 100 ml or 100 gm.
6. Opium preparations - Not more than 100 mg per 100 ml or 100 gm (Parepectolin, Kapectolin PG, Kaolin Pectin P.G.).
7. Lyrica - Pregabalin
8. Vimpat - Lacosamide
9. Potiga – Ezogabine

EMERGENCY DISPENSING OF SCHEDULE II CONTROLLED DRUGS

1. In case of an emergency situation, a pharmacist may dispense a controlled substance listed in Schedule II upon receiving an orally or electronically transmitted authorization of a prescribing practitioner, provided that:

2. The quantity prescribed and dispensed shall be limited to the amount adequate to treat the patient during the emergency period.

3. The prescription contains all information required by the federal and state law except for the actual signature of the prescribing practitioner, and in the case of an oral prescription, or prescription transmitted electronically by computer modem or other similar electronic device, the prescription is immediately reduced to writing by the dispensing pharmacist; and

4. The dispensing pharmacist makes a reasonable good faith effort to determine that the orally or electronically transmitted authorization was issued by an authorized practitioner, which effort may include a callback to the prescribing practitioner or other good faith efforts to ensure the prescribing practitioner's identity.

5. Within seven days after authorizing an emergency oral prescription, the prescribing practitioner shall cause a written prescription for the emergency quantity prescribed to be delivered to the pharmacy which must have written on its face "Authorization for Emergency Dispensing" and should comply with federal and state law.

6. Upon receipt of the written prescription, the dispensing pharmacist shall attach the prescription to the orally or electronically transmitted emergency prescription which had earlier been reduced to writing.

7. The pharmacist must notify the nearest office of the Administration if the prescribing individual practitioner fails to deliver a written prescription to him/her; failure of the pharmacist to do so shall void the authority conferred by this paragraph to dispense without a written prescription of a prescribing individual practitioner.

FAXING SCHEDULE II CONTROLLED DRUGS

A prescription for a Schedule II controlled substance may be transmitted by the practitioner or the agent of the practitioner, but not by the patient or patient's agent, to a pharmacy via facsimile equipment, provided the original written, signed prescription is presented to the pharmacist for review prior to the actual dispensing of the controlled substance.

Faxing Prescription For Schedule II Controlled Drugs May Serve As The Original Prescription Only If:

1. A prescription is written for a Schedule II narcotic substance to be compounded for the direct administration to a patient by parenteral, intravenous, intramuscular, subcutaneous or intraspinal infusion may be transmitted by the practitioner or the practitioner's agent to the pharmacy by facsimile.

2. A prescription is written for Schedule II substance for the resident of the Long Term Care Facility may be transmitted by the practitioner or the practitioner's agent to the dispensing pharmacy by facsimile.

3. A prescription is written for a Schedule II narcotic substance for a patient enrolled in the hospice care program certified and/or paid for by Medicare under Title XVIII or a hospice program which is licensed by the state may be transmitted by the practitioner or the practitioner's agent to the dispensing pharmacy by facsimile. The practitioner or the practitioner's agent will note on the prescription that the patient is the hospice patient.

METHADONE DISPENSING

1. A practitioner who wants to use Schedule II narcotic drugs for maintenance and/or detoxification must obtain separate registration from DEA as a narcotic treatment program pursuant to the Narcotic Addict Treatment Act of 1974.

2. This registration allows a practitioner to administer or dispense, but NOT PRESCRIBE, scheduled narcotic drugs that are approved by the United States Food and Drug Administration (FDA) for the treatment of narcotic addiction. Methadone, Buprenorphine and levo-alpha-acetyl-methadol (LAAM) are the scheduled narcotics approved by FDA for use in maintenance and detoxification treatment.

3. An exception to the registration requirement, known as the "three day rule" (21CFR1306.07(b)), allows a practitioner who is not separately registered as a narcotic treatment program, to administer (but not prescribe) narcotic drugs to a patient for the purpose of relieving acute withdrawal symptoms while arranging for the patient's referral for treatment, under the following conditions:

a. Not more than one day's medication may be administered or given to a patient at one time;
b. This treatment may not be carried out for more than 72 hours and;
c. This 72-hour period cannot be renewed or extended.

4. The 72-hour exception offers an opioid dependent individual relief from experiencing acute withdrawal symptoms, while the physician arranges placement in a maintenance/detoxification treatment program. This provision was established to augment, not to circumvent, the separate registration requirement.

MANAGING OPIOID ADDICTION WITH BUPRENORPHINE

Legislation has enabled physicians to treat opioid-dependent patients with an office-based maintenance program using buprenorphine, a partial mu-opioid receptor agonist. Clinical studies indicate buprenorphine effectively manages opioid addiction. Buprenorphine prescribed for addiction requires the practitioner to have an "X" Drug Enforcement Administration (DEA) number.

Buprenorphine is more effective than placebo for managing opioid addiction but may not be superior to methadone if high doses are needed. It is comparable to lower doses of methadone, however.

Treatment phases include induction, stabilization, and maintenance. Buprenorphine therapy should be initiated at the onset of withdrawal symptoms and adjusted to address withdrawal symptoms and cravings. Advantages of buprenorphine include low abuse potential and high availability for office use.

Disadvantages include high cost and possible lack of effectiveness in patients who require high methadone doses. Most family physicians are required to complete eight hours of training before they can prescribe buprenorphine for opioid addiction.

FILING METHODS FOR CONTROLLED SUBSTANCES

A. One file for CII,
Second file for CIII, CIV and CV,
Third file for non-controlled substances.

B. One file for CII,
Second file for CIII, CIV, CV and non-controlled substances.

C. One file for CII, CIII, CIV and CV with the condition that all III, IV and V should be previously marked "C" with red ink on face of the prescription, so that it can be easily differentiated from CII,
Second file of non-controlled substance.

DESTRUCTION/THEFT OF CONTROLLED DRUGS

The request to destroy controlled substances should be done by filling a DEA 41 form. If the institution has a past history of very low drug abuse, the DEA may authorize registrant to destroy the drug without the DEA representative.

OR

The drugs that need to be destroyed can be forwarded to the state agency.

OR

The drugs that need to be destroyed can be forwarded to the DEA field office.

The theft of CII drugs should be immediately reported to the DEA office or local police.

A report of theft must be made on the DEA 106 form.

DEA 222 ORDER FORM

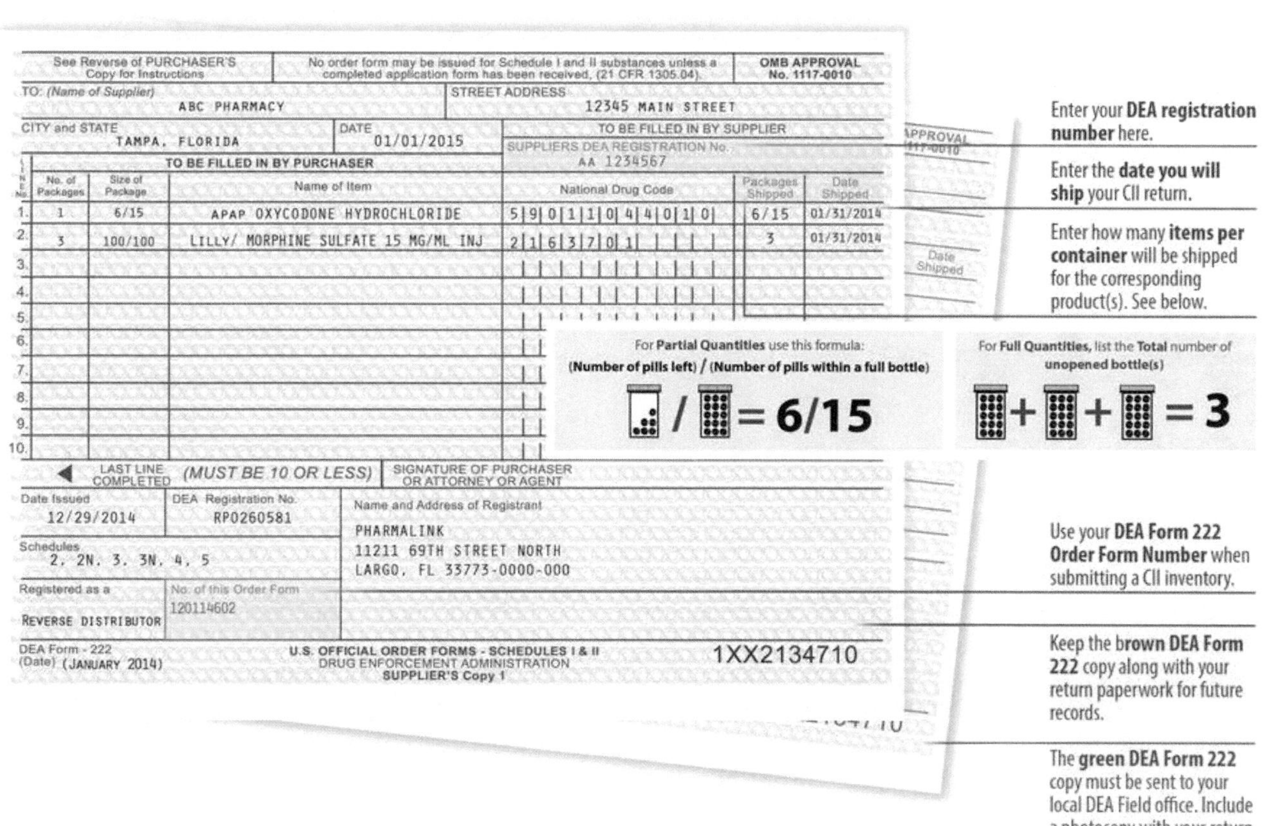

1. This form must be used to order CI or CII drugs.
2. Each order form contains three copies. Copy I, Copy II and Copy III.
3. There are ten lines on each order form. Only one item can be entered on one line. For each item, one must include name of the drug (Ritalin), the dosage form of the drug (tablet) and the volume or unit of the drug in each container (# 100).
4. Copy III should be kept by the person filling out the DEA form. Copy I and II should be submitted to the supplier.
5. The supplier records the date and quantity shipped to the purchaser on Copy I and II. Copy II is sent to the DEA by supplier and Copy I should be kept by supplier for his own record.
6. Upon receiving the order form from the supplier, the purchaser must record all the received items on the appropriate line with date received.
7. Any partial supply of the drug must be filled by supplier within 60 days from the order date.

ELECTRONIC DEA 222 ORDER FORM

To be valid, the purchaser must sign an electronic order for a Schedule I or II controlled substance with a digital signature issued to the purchaser, or the purchaser's agent, by DEA.

The following data fields must be included on an electronic order for Schedule I and II controlled substances:

1. A unique number the purchaser assigns to track the order. The number must be in the following 9-character format: the last two digits of the year, X, and six characters as selected by the purchaser.
2. The purchaser's DEA registration number.
3. The name of the supplier.
4. The complete address of the supplier (may be completed by either the purchaser or the supplier).
5. The supplier's DEA registration number (may be completed by either the purchaser or the supplier).
6. The date the order is signed.
7. The name (including strength where appropriate) of the controlled substance product or the National Drug Code (NDC) number (the NDC number may be completed by either the purchaser or the supplier).
8. The quantity in a single package or container.

9. The number of packages or containers of each item ordered.

10. An electronic order may include controlled substances that are not in schedules I and II and non-controlled substances.

DIGITAL CERTIFICATE

1. The following persons are eligible to obtain a CSOS digital certificate from the DEA Certification Authority to sign electronic orders for controlled substances.

2. The person who signed the most recent DEA registration application or renewal application and a person authorized to sign a registration application.

3. A person granted power of attorney by the DEA registrant to sign orders for one or more schedules of controlled substances.

4. A CSOS digital certificate issued by the DEA Certification Authority will authorize the certificate holder to sign orders for only those schedules of controlled substances covered by the registration under which the certificate is issued.

5. When a registrant, in a power of attorney letter, limits a certificate applicant to a subset of the registrant's authorized schedules, the registrant is responsible for ensuring that the certificate holder signs orders only for that subset of schedules.

TO CHECK VALIDITY OF DEA NUMBER

The DEA number is nine characters consisting of two letters followed by seven numbers.

The first letter generally gives an idea about the registrant. If person is a prescriber then it would begin with an (A) or a (B); if it is a mid-level prescriber then it would begin with an (M). If it is a distributor then it would begin with a (P) or (R).

The second letter is usually the first letter of the last name of registrant.

The rest of the six characters are computer generated, unique for each registrant. The last seventh digit is the key to verifying the validity of the DEA number.

TO VERIFY A DEA NUMBER

1. Add the first, third and fifth number of the DEA number.

2. Add the second, fourth and sixth number of the DEA number and multiply the resultant sum by two.

3. Add the resultant sums of (II) to (I).

4. The final most right number of this sum should match with the ninth digit of the provider DEA number.

For example, Dr. Ayan Shroff with DEA # BS 2435786 can be verified by:

The first letter "B" indicates the prescriber.
The second letter should be the first initial of the last name of prescriber; therefore it should be "S" in this case.

Now adding the first, third and fifth digits of given DEA number will give us 2 + 3 + 7 = 12.

Now adding the second, fourth and six digits of given DEA number will give us 4 + 5 + 8 = 17.
Now multiply the resultant sum of second, fourth and sixth digits by "2' (17 x 2 = 34)
Now add this sum to the sum of the first, third and fifth digits of the DEA number: 12 + 34 = 46.

The number 6 (the final most right number of sum) is matching with the last number of the provider's DEA number BS 2435786, and therefore the given DEA number is valid.

34. The Health Insurance Portability and Accountability Act of 1996

The Health Insurance Portability and Accountability Act of 1996 (HIPAA) was signed into law on August 21, 1996. This law includes important new protection for millions of working Americans and their families who have pre-existing medical conditions or might suffer discrimination in health coverage based on a factor that relates to an individual's health.

The HIPAA legislation had four primary objectives:

1. Assure health insurance portability by eliminating job-lock due to pre-existing medical conditions
2. Reduce healthcare fraud and abuse
3. Enforce standards for health information
4. Guarantee security and privacy of health information

The HIPAA legislation is organized as follows:

Title I:

1. Guarantees health insurance access, portability and renewal
2. Guarantees coverage and renewal
3. Eliminates some preexisting condition exclusions
4. Prohibits discrimination based on health status

Title II:

1. Preventing healthcare fraud and abuse
2. Fraud and abuse controls
3. Administrative Simplification (AS) provisions (Subtitle)
4. Medical Liability Reform

Title III:

1. Medical Savings Accounts
2. Health Insurance tax deduction for self-employed

Title IV:

1. Enforcement of group health plan provisions

Out of these four titles, we will discuss Title I in detail.

HIPAA's provisions amend Title I of the Employee Retirement Income Security Act of 1974 (ERISA) as well as the Internal Revenue Code and the Public Health Service Act, and place requirements on employer-sponsored group health plans, insurance companies and health maintenance organizations (HMOs).

HIPAA Title I has included the following regulations:

1. Limit exclusions for pre-existing conditions.

2. Prohibit discrimination against employees and dependents based on their health status.

3. Guarantee renewability and availability of health coverage to certain employers and individuals.

4. Protect many workers who lose health coverage by providing better access to individual health insurance coverage.

Under HIPAA, a group health plan or a health insurance issuer offering group health insurance coverage may impose pre-existing condition exclusion with respect to a participant or beneficiary only if the following requirements are satisfied:

1. Pre-existing condition exclusion must relate to a condition for which medical advice, diagnosis, care or treatment was recommended or received during the 6-month period prior to an individual's enrollment date;

2. Pre-existing condition exclusion may not last for more than 12 months (18 months for late enrollees) after an individual's enrollment date.

3. This 12 or 18-month period must be reduced by the number of days of the individual's prior creditable coverage, excluding coverage before any break in coverage of 63 days or more.

Currently some employer health plans do not cover pre-existing medical conditions. HIPAA limits the time period of these restrictions so that most plans must cover an individual's pre-existing condition after 12 months.

Under HIPAA, a new employer's plan will be required to give you credit for the length of time that person had continuous health coverage that will reduce the 12-month exclusion period. If, at the time employees change jobs, they already have had 12 months of continuous health coverage (without a break in coverage of 63 days or more), they will not have to start over with a new 12- month exclusion for any pre-existing conditions.

The "pre-existing condition" is defined as a condition present before a person's enrollment date in any new health plan. Under HIPAA, the only pre-existing conditions that may be excluded under the pre-existing condition exclusion are those for which medical advice, diagnosis, care or treatment was recommended or received within the 6-month period ending on the enrollment date.

If an employee had a medical condition in the past, but has not received any medical advice, diagnosis, care or treatment within the 6 months prior to the enrollment date in the plan, his old condition is not a "pre-existing condition" for which exclusion can be applied.

State Requirement and HIPAA

States may impose stricter obligations on health insurance issuers in the areas listed below. States may:

1. Shorten the 6-month "look-back" period prior to the enrollment date to determine what pre-existing condition is.

2. Shorten the 12- and 18-month maximum pre-existing condition exclusion periods.

3. Increase the 63-day significant break in coverage period.

4. Increase the 30-day period for newborns, adopted children and children placed for adoption to enroll in the plan so that no pre-existing condition exclusion period may be applied thereafter.

5. Expand the prohibitions on conditions and people to whom a pre-existing condition exclusion period may be applied beyond the "exceptions" described in federal law (the "exceptions" under federal law are for certain newborns, adopted children, children placed for adoption and pregnancy).

6. Require additional special enrollment periods.

7. Reduce the maximum HMO affiliation period to less than 2 months (3 months for late enrollees).

Therefore, if person's health coverage is offered through an HMO or an insurance policy issued by an insurance company, he/she should check with his/her State Insurance Commissioner's Office to find out the rules in the state.

35. Interpersonal Communication

Interpersonal Communication: It is a common but complex practice that is essential in dealing with patients and other healthcare providers.

There are five major components that affect the interpersonal communications model. They are:

1. Sender
2. Message
3. Receiver
4. Feedback
5. Barriers

1. **Sender:** The sender transmits a message to another person.

2. **Message:** The message is the element that is transmitted from one person to another. Message can be thoughts, ideas, emotions, information, or other factors that can be transmitted verbally and nonverbally.

3. **Receiver:** The receiver receives the message from the sender.

4. **Feedback:** It is the process in which the initial receiver is communicating back to the initial sender to understand the sender's message.

5. **Barriers:** These are interferences that may affect the accuracy of the communication exchange. For example, a telephone rings in background, loud noise, in-store announcements etc.

Perception and Communication

Perception is one of the most important elements in the communication process. In interpersonal communication, a message is transformed from the sender to the receiver. The most important thing about this transmitted message is how the transmitted message is interpreted by the receiver.

The sender delivers the message, but the receiver may not interpret its meaning in the same way as the sender intended. At this point, a perception comes into effect. The receiver normally determines the meaning based on the perception of the individual sending the message.

For example, MS comes to a pharmacy and complains about side effects caused by a Nitroglycerine patch prescribed to him. The directions on prescription say "apply one patch daily." Upon detailed conversation with him, the pharmacist has found 20 patches on his body. MS did not perceive that "apply one patch daily" meant that he should remove an old patch before applying the new patch on the body.

Persuasion and Credibility

Many times, a pharmacist has to persuade a patient to make a correct decision. For example, when a patient is on antibiotics, he has to convince the patient to take the full 14-day course of treatment. Here, the pharmacist is persuading his patient through his professional credibility, known as perceived credibility.

Credibility is defined as an element that influences people's thinking and behavior. People are influenced more by those whom they believe are credible. For example, a speech on diabetes-related issues conducted by a pharmacy student and diabetic-expert practitioner - the audience will be more influenced by the speech of the practitioner over the pharmacy student because of his credibility.

Perceived Credibility Is Influenced By Three Major Factors:

1. A Safety or Trustworthiness Element
2. An Expertness or Qualification Element
3. A Personal or Dynamism Element

1. **A Safety or Trustworthiness Element**: The trustworthiness factor is associated with worth, friendliness, and sociability that enhances the perception of an individual being "safe" to talk. For example, if a pharmacist is friendly and trustworthy, patients may also seek non-health related advises such as home mortgage finance, choosing the right college or buying a car.

2. **An Expertness or Qualification Element:** The expertness factor assures the receiver that the sender has sufficient background knowledge and experience about a topic. For example, the audience may not be influenced by the speech of the pharmacist on heart-related surgery since it is not his expertise.

3. **A Personal or Dynamism Element**: The personal dynamism factor may influence the receiver by the sender's overall personality and characteristics.

Nonverbal Communication And Its Elements

The process of interpersonal communication involves both verbal and nonverbal expressions. Nonverbal communication involves different types of behaviors, psychological responses, and environmental interactions through which we consciously or unconsciously relate to another person.

Nonverbal communication is important for two reasons.

1. It mirrors the innermost thoughts and feelings of the sender.
2. Unlike verbal communication, it is difficult to "fake."

There are few important elements of nonverbal communication. These are:

1. Kinesics (body movement)
2. Proxemics (distance between communicators)
4. Physical Environment
5. Distracting Nonverbal Components

1. **Kinesics (Body Movement):** The manner in which one uses his arms, legs, hands, head, or face may have a dramatic effect on the message he sends. Handshaking is a perfect example of kinesics. By handshaking with another person, a sender is passing a nonverbal message of friendship to the receiver. This is really important when health care provider serving to patients. A patient sometimes feels shy or uncomfortable about disclosing or sharing certain information with pharmacists or prescribers and at that time kinesics plays an important role. How one generates the feeling of empathy and creating comfort zone should be the key to dealing with such patients.

There are two types of kinesics (Body Postures):

1. Open Posture
2. Closed Posture

1. **Open Posture:** Sincerity, respect, and empathy for the patient can be nonverbally communicated by an "open posture." The perfect example of an open posture is standing with a full frontal appearance to the person with whom you are interacting. As an open communicator, the pharmacist should have his legs comfortably apart, not crossed, arms at the side with the palms of the hands facing front, and a facial expression indicating interest and a willingness to listen as well as speak.

A list of expressions helps to communicate through an open posture:

1. Relaxed posture
2. Varied eye contact (consistent, but not a stare)
3. Frontal appearance
4. Slight lean toward the other person
5. Erect body position (head up, shoulders back)
6. Comfortable and appropriate gestures
7. Facilitating movements of legs and hands

Out of these, we briefly discuss eye contact and vocal qualities here.

1A. **Eye contact**: Facial expressions are assumed to reveal personality traits. A great deal of information is communicated through head and facial movements, but the person's eyes provide more clues than any other facial expressions. Therefore, a gaze is classified as a major nonverbal signal to others.

For successful communication, a pharmacist should have frequent and attentive eye contact with the patient, but avoid just blank stares. Eye contact helps pharmacists to convey the message to the patient that "I am listening."

1B. **Vocal qualities:** Pitch, range, tone, clarity and tempo are classified as vocal qualities. Pitch refers to frequency level of voice. Pitch level influences patient attitudes toward pharmacists and the content of the message.
Voice clarity is also an important element for effective communication. Pharmacists must speak clearly and audibly in order to successfully communicate with patients. Tempo is the speed of vocal production. Inappropriate silences and delays may irritate the patient and result in a poor communication. Fast tempos with frequent pauses are often associated with emotions such as fear or anger. Slow tempos are also associated with anger, however sometimes it may be due to depression, sadness or a lack of confidence. A slow tempo with frequent pauses and utterances like "uh," "er" and "um" normally indicate a patient's uncertainly.

2. **Closed Posture:** A closed posture is adopted by a person who does not wish to continue communication. The expressions involve legs crossed at the knees, head facing downward, eyes looking at the floor and arms folded in front of the chest. Any time during conversation, if any of the parties adopts this posture, it indicates unwillingness to continue communication. Communication from a closed posture is shortens or halts further productive interaction between parties.

2. **Proxemics:** The distance between two interacting persons plays an important role in communication. It is a powerful nonverbal communication tool. It has been found those different distances between communication transforms different nonverbal messages to another party. The most protected space is that from full contact to 18 inches from our bodies. This space or distance is reserved for others with whom we have a close or intimate relationship. When any stranger or person with whom we are not intimate with enters into this (intimate) zone, we feel anxiety, frustration and even anger.

A crowded elevator represents the example of proxemics. People in crowded elevator will do almost anything to avoid touching one another. If by chance two parties do have bodily contact, they usually make profuse apologies even though neither of them have space to avoid contact with each other.

In normal circumstances, the distance maintained between two communicators engaged in a social interaction ranges from 4 to 12 feet. Interpersonal distances greater than 12 feet are reserved or usually seen when one person is speaking and others are listening as an audience.

Every pharmacist or health provider should consider and obey the factor of distance. For example, during counseling if you trespass frequently into a patient's intimate zone, you are taking a risk. Therefore, it is really important for a pharmacist, when counseling a patient, to stand close enough to ensure privacy, yet at the same time provide sufficient room for the patient so that he/she does not feel uncomfortable.

3. **Environmental Nonverbal Factors:** A number of environmental factors may affect the nonverbal message sent to patients. The color, lighting, and use of the pharmacy are important environmental factors that may affect nonverbal communication between pharmacists and patients. The most discussed environmental factor of the typical pharmacy design is its prescription counter. It has been described as a major barrier in initiating interpersonal communication with patients. It has been preferred by those pharmacists who fear or try to avoid interpersonal communication with patients.

Other factors such as cleanliness of the pharmacy, an organized medication shelf or a cleanliness of prescription counter pass on important nonverbal messages to patients. Another environmental factor that affects most is the professional dress code of pharmacists and technicians. A pharmacist must dress professionally in order to convey assertiveness and professional competence to patients.

4. **Distracting Nonverbal Components:** One of the most common barriers in nonverbal communication is lack of eye contact with the patient. It is frustrating for a patient to talk with a pharmacist who is not looking at him. Many times, it has been observed that unintentionally the pharmacist avoids looking at a patient when talking to him. During conversation he looks at the prescription, the prescription container, or other object, but not at the patient. This passes the message to the patient that the pharmacist is not confident about what he is saying or is just ignoring him.

The second most distracting nonverbal component is the facial expressions of the pharmacist. For example, while talking with the patient, if the pharmacist's eyes roll or move frequently toward other objects, it conveys the message of no concern or lack of interest.

The third most important distracting nonverbal component is the body position of the pharmacist. Patients normally read or sense a willingness to talk to them based on their perception of body position.

The fourth and last distracting nonverbal component is the pharmacist's tone of voice. Patients interpret messages not only through words but also through the tone or type of voice used to convey messages. An inappropriate tone of voice can upset patients and may create entirely different meanings of the message.

Barriers In Communications

During communication, there are numerous barriers that may affect or disturb personal interaction. There barriers can be divided into five major categories:

1. Environmental Barriers
2. Personal Barriers
3. Patient Barriers
4. Administrative and Financial Barriers
5. Time Barriers

1. **Environmental Barriers:** Distractions related to the environment often interfere with the process of communication. One of the most obvious barriers in this category is the height of the prescription counter separating the patient from the pharmacist. In certain stores, it is so high that even the patient cannot see the pharmacist. This type of environment may give patients the impression that the pharmacist does not want to talk to them.

Crowded and noisy prescription areas are the second biggest obstruction for communication between a patient and pharmacist. Cash register ringing, music playing in the back ground, telephone ringing or people talking may play major role in limiting communication between the pharmacist and patient.

Another subtle barrier is the pharmacist's desire to answer every call, which gives the impression that the pharmacist is not willing to talk to the patient.

2. **Personal Barriers:** Lack of confidence in personal communication or low self-esteem may act as a major barrier in interpersonal communication. Another barrier in this category is the degree of personal shyness. Individuals with high shyness levels tend to avoid interpersonal communication in most situations. These types of people have a high level of fear or anxiety associated with communicating with other people.

Another type of personal barrier in communication is talking to yourself (internal conversation) while communicating with others. For example, while you are listening to somebody, you may ask yourself whether you want to deal with this person or not. This will distract you from your normal communication. Another personal barrier that may interfere with the communication process is the transference of the problem to another person. For example, you may say to your technician to take care of a patient since you are really busy filling prescriptions. Cross-cultural factors also categorize under the persona barriers. For example, in some cultures, it is disrespectful to engage in eye contact during communication.

Another personal barrier that limits the communication is the fear of being in a situation that is sensitive or difficult to handle. For example, when an HIV patient expresses the fear of dying, we do not know how to communicate with him. The last barrier in this category is that many pharmacists believe that talking with patients is not a high priority activity.

3. **Patient Behavior:** These are communication barriers from the pharmacist's perspective. There are several barriers that may prevent patients from communicating with the pharmacist. The most important one is the perception about the pharmacist. If the patient perceives that the pharmacist is not knowledgeable, then he will avoid communicating with the pharmacist. Also, if the patient perceives that the pharmacist does not want to talk to him, he will not initiate communication. Thus the patient's perception about the pharmacist plays an important role in initiating communication with the pharmacist.

   Another example of patient perception is their belief about the healthcare system. Many of them believe that the healthcare system is impersonal, and caregivers are not concerned about them as individuals but rather as cases or disease state. This type of hidden belief may also act as a barrier in interpersonal communication.

   A patient's perception of their medical condition may also act as a barrier in the communication process. Many times patients believe that their condition is relatively minor and they do not require counseling or consultation with anybody beside their physician. In contrast, patients may be really worried and anxious about their medical condition and not want to talk with anybody. Also, there is a belief among many patients that they should not know anything more than what is stated on the prescription container.

4. **Administrative And Financial Barriers:** There are several administrative and financial factors that prevent or act as barriers in the process of communication. Since pharmacists are not getting any incentive to counsel the patient, they try to spend their time filling prescriptions or with other activities which may provide them financial incentives. For example, many pharmacies provide an annual bonus to their pharmacists on the basis of the number of prescriptions filled or number of formulary prescriptions dispensed.

   The second factor that prevents the pharmacist from communicating with the patient is workload and a limited number of staff members. Since the profession of the pharmacist is well reimbursed by pharmacies, many pharmacy managers do not want their pharmacists to spend time counseling patients. Also cost containment strategies of pharmacies may offer less help to pharmacists, though cutting down staffing members may act as a principal barrier in interpersonal communication with patients.

5. **Time Barriers:** Trying to initiate communication at an inappropriate time may also lead to communication failure. For example, a patient has just come from the dentist office where he has waited for 2 hours to have removed his wisdom teeth. He is at the pharmacy to get his pain medication filled and may not be in a condition to communicate. The same way if the pharmacist has lots of prescriptions to fill, he will not be able to communicate with the patient; if he communicates, he cannot provide a reasonable time for successful counseling.

Assertiveness

There are generally three types of behaviors we commonly see in practical life. These are:

1. Passive Behavior
2. Aggressive Behavior
3. Assertive Behavior

1. **Passive Behavior:** This type of behavior is adopted by a nonassertive person in order to avoid conflict. Persons who adopt this type of behavior will not say what they think or express their opinion because of fear of others. The passive person "hides" from people and waits for others to initiate conversation.

2. **Aggressive Behavior:** This type of behavior is normally seen by people who seek to "win" in conflict situations by dominating or initiating others. This person tries to promote his own interests or point of view and does not respect other people's feelings, ideas or needs.

3. **Assertive Behavior:** The third type of behavior (ideal behavior) is an assertive behavior. It is a type of response that focuses on resolving conflict in relationships in an atmosphere of mutual respect. It is defined as the direct expression of ideas, opinions, and desires. The assertive individual initiates communication in a way that conveys concern and respect for others. To be assertive, each person tries to convey the message through "This is what I think," "This is how I feel about your presentation," or "This is what I think we should do." The major factor in being assertive is the ability to present without being an offensive to other people's ideas, thoughts or their needs. It is required that pharmacists should follow assertive behavior when communicating with patients.

Components For Successful Interview

Conducting a successful and effective interview is a hard task. The interview process contains several critical components that need to be mastered. There are a few important components for successful interview skills. These are:

1. Listening
2. Probing
3. Use of silence
4. Establishing rapport

1. **Listening:** Most times we see people who are better senders of information than receivers of information. We have been taught to be good speakers or writers, but rarely we are good listeners. Therefore, we have to more concentrate on listening part of communication process. Nothing will end an interview faster than having a patient realize that you are not listening to them. Therefore, good listening skills are inevitably required by pharmacists to conduct successful communication.

2. **Probing:** It is another important communication skill. It is defined as the art of asking questions in order to get the most accurate information from the patient. Asking questions to patients requires skill. Several things should be considered before asking questions to patients. Among them, the phrasing of questions is the most important. Patients often react to questions which seem to describe them as ill.

   For example: "Why are you taking these medications?" The question's tone is more toward authority or seeking explanation from patients. These types of questions must be avoided. Instead of this, one can ask, "For what reason are you taking these medications?"

   To conduct a successful interview, one must also know the difference between open- ended and close-ended questions. The answers for close-ended questions generally end with either "yes" or "no." This type of question does not require a detailed explanation.
   For example, "Has your doctor started this new medication just recently?" The patient may respond with a "yes" or "no." In contrast, open-ended questions neither limit the patient's response nor induce

defensiveness. For example, "When did your doctor start this new medication?" The phrasing of this question asks for detailed explanations from the patient about the introduction of new medication in the patient's regimen.

Most of the times we see more closed-ended questions in the interview process and therefore they are also known as "patient-centered questions." The advantages of closed-ended questions are:

1. They reduce the patient's degree of openness.
2. They enable patients to avoid specific subjects and emotional expression.

However, open-ended questions are less likely to cause misunderstanding, and may promote rapport and develop trusting and long-lasting relationships.

3. **Use of Silence**: This is another skill that pharmacists should learn in order to successfully conduct communication. Many times before initiating communication, small period of silence exists. The pharmacist must be patient and adopt this pause as a part of communication.

Also, many times, the patient needs time to think and gather information about the question being asked. At that time, interrupting the silence distracts the patient's concentration and may result in poor communication.

4. **Establishing Rapport**: This is the factor that measures the outcome of the interview. Its seen that most successful interviews may lead to a high degree of rapport between a patient and pharmacist. The base of rapport mainly depends on mutual consideration and respect from both parties. By being sincere, friendly, trustworthy and courteous during the discussion, the pharmacist can build a long-lasting and friendly relationship with the patient.

36. New Drug Approval Process

No new drug can be legally marketed in the U.S. without approval by the FDA.

The innovator company must submit an IND (Notice of Claimed Investigational Exemption for a New Drug) for approval. After an approval of IND from the FDA, the manufacturer may then conduct clinical studies of its investigational new drug.

The Law Requires The Manufacturer To Submit The Following Information:

1. The name of the drug
2. Its composition
3. Methods of manufacturing and quality control
4. Information from preclinical investigations regarding pharmacological, pharmacokinetic, and toxicological evaluation.

The FDA may answer within 30 days from the date the IND is filled. If the FDA approves the IND, the innovator company may start human clinical testing of the new drug.

The Testing Proceeds Through Three Different Phases:

1. Phase I clinical trial
2. Phase II clinical trial
3. Phase III clinical trial

1. **Phase I Trial:** The purpose of phase I clinical trial is to detect the adverse effects of the new drug.

This phase involves a small number of subjects for the study of the drug's toxicity, bioavailability, metabolism, elimination and pharmacological action of the drug.

Initially, a number of subjects receives a low dose of the new drug, which is gradually increased once safety of the new drug is assured.

2. **Phase II Trial:** The new drug is now tested on a limited number of patients who actually suffers from the disease for which the new drug is claimed for. Phase II clinical trial helps to determine the efficacy of the drug and dosage at which efficacy may occur.

3. **Phase III Trial:** This trial involves hundreds or thousands of patients. The study is often conducted at physicians' offices or hospitals that have contracted with the manufacturer to conduct studies.

A Double Blind Study is normally conducted in this phase. It is the type of study in which the nature of the drug is concealed from patients as well as attending physicians. In this type of study, one group of patients receives the testing drug and the other group of patients receives the placebo; the results of both groups are then compared to find out the true effectiveness of the drug. If the phase III studies are favorable, the drug sponsors may submit an NDA to the FDA.

The NDA contains the complete report including the drug's safety and efficacy which has been noted on the IND.

By law the FDA has 180 days to review the NDA and answer the sponsor's company.

4. **Phase IV Trial:** It is also known as the postmarketing surveillance.

Once the new drug application has been approved, the innovator company may legally distribute the drug in interstate commerce.

Manufacturers must maintain and keep adequate postmarketing reports and records.

Manufacturers must submit any new information regarding the drug's safety and efficacy or any serious drug interactions to the FDA.

The Importance of Postmarketing Surveillance:

1. To compare the drug's safety and effectiveness in a vast range or group of patients.

2. To find out the long-term aspects of toxicity and adverse effects of the newly introduced drug.

37. Clinical Drug-Literature

It is defined as an extensive, heterogenous collection of resources which provides information about drugs.

Drug Information Sources Can Be Classified Into Three Important Categories:

1. Primary literature
2. Secondary literature
3. Tertiary literature

Primary Literature: Articles appearing in pharmaceutical or medical journals have the most current and accurate health related information. They are classified as primary literature.

Advantage of Primary Literature:

1. The most current and accurate drug and health related information.

Disadvantages of Primary Literature:

1. They are the least feasible to pharmacists, pharmacy students or physicians.

Secondary Literature: It represents two types of resources:

a. Indexing (bibliographic)
b. Abstracting

They represent the most expensive investment of literate library.

Several considerations should be applied before selecting the secondary sources:

1. Lag Time
2. Coverage of Literature
3. Selectivity of Indexing And Abstracting
4. Cost

1. Lag Time: It is defined as time elapsed between documents published in journals versus when it was first abstracted or indexed. The article with a prolonged lag time may lack the updated or current information.

2. Coverage Of Literature/Selectivity Of Indexing And Abstracting: One should pay close attention when selecting secondary literature from journals. For example, pharmacy-related journals are less likely to provide article information on cardiac or neurosurgery.

3. Cost: The drug information is available from different sources. For example: cd rom, standard print, website or microfiche. These various sources may have different cost. It is therefore very important to evaluate individual needs at the practice site and purchase accordingly.

Advantage Of Secondary Literature:

1. More current and updated information compared to tertiary literature.

Disadvantages Of Secondary Literature:

1. Less current and updated information compared to primary literature.
2. Very expensive.

Tertiary Literature: Reference books and textbooks are considered as tertiary literatures.

Advantage Of Tertiary Literature:

1. Easy accessibility
2. Less expensive

Disadvantages Of Tertiary Literature:

1. Lack of current or updated information.
2. The author may interpret information incorrectly from the primary source, and may provide inaccurate information.

Classification of Drug Information Sources:

A. Parenteral

1. Handbook of Injectable drugs
2. Guide to Parenteral Admixture

B. Poison Information Resources

1. Dreisbach's Handbook of Poisoning
2. Clinical Toxicology of Commercial Products

D. Drug Manufacture Outside of USA

1. Index Nominum
2. Martindale: The Extra Pharmacopoeia
3. USAN Dictionary of Drugs Names
4. USP Dictionary of Drugs Names

E. Product Orientated References

1. American Drug Index
2. PDR
3. Facts and Comparisons
4. Handbook of Nonprescription Drugs
5. Blue book
6. Red book

C. **Adverse Effects**

1. Textbook of ADR
2. Side effects of drug

F. **Investigational Drugs**

1. The NDA Pipeline
2. Drug Facts and Comparisons
3. Martindale: The Extra Pharmacopoeia

G. **Drug Orientated References**

1. AHFS Drug Information
2. USP Dispensing Information
3. AMA Drug Evaluation
4. Martindale: The Extra Pharmacopoeia
5. Pharmacological Basis of Therapeutics

H. **Therapeutic Orientated References**

1. Merck Manual
2. Applied Therapeutics
3. Clinical Pharmacy and Therapeutics
4. Cancer Chemotherapy Handbook

I. **Dispensing Orientated References**

1. USP-NF
2. Merck Index
3. Remington

38. Poison Control and Accidental Poisoning

A poison is any substance that can cause harm to your body. Accidental poisoning is common. In spite of all the recent advances, the number of ingestions and/or exposures to household medications and chemicals continues to climb. About 1 million children 5 and younger are exposed to potentially poisonous substances each year, according to a 2001 report from the Centers of Disease Control and Prevention (CDC). And about 25 die.

Protecting children from toxic exposure to drugs, chemicals and other potential household hazards is an important role for parents. Poison prevention begins by educating parents, grandparents and others who take care of our children, about what types of substances can be harmful to children. We must learn to think from a child's perspective and viewpoint when considering how the home environment may pose potential risks that could lead to accidental poisoning. Also, adults must know where and how to get help for poisonings when needed.

Childhood poisoning is a preventable injury. Efforts aimed at preventing accidental poisoning have to take into consideration the developmental age of the child. Children ages 1 to 3 are at highest risk for accidental poisoning because they may put anything into their mouths. Children at this age are just beginning to become mobile and many things in the home are now easily accessible to them. Childproofing measures in the home are best initiated when the child is 6 months of age or before the child becomes mobile.

Children who are 3 to 5 years old will frequently eat any pills they discover. These children are normally curious youngsters, and they also like to mimic adult behaviors. As children get closer to adolescence, poison prevention efforts need to shift from protection to education. Family discussions about the dangers of alcohol and other drugs should begin in the home. Remember, adult behavior serves as an example to adolescents who are beginning to assert independence and start making more decisions on their own.

According to the AAPCC database, the substance most frequently involved in human poisoning exposures are cleaning substances, followed by analgesics, cosmetics, plants, cough and cold preparations, hydrocarbons, bites, topicals, foreign bodies, pesticides, foods and sedative/hypnotics/antipsychotics.

In contrast, the most frequent category of toxic substances involved in reported fatalities were antidepressants, followed by analgesics, stimulants, street drugs, cardiovascular drugs, sedative/hypnotics, gases, fumes, chemicals, alcohol, asthma therapies, cleaning substances and hydrocarbons.

Factors Affecting Accidental Poisoning:

1. Age
2. Accidental proneness
3. Location
4. Accessibility
5. Type of container

1. **Age:** Approximately two-thirds of poisonings that occur in children are accidental. The most critical age period is between 1 and 3 years. During this period, one-half of the poisonings occur.

2. **Accidental Proneness**: It is rare. Normally in this type, children treated for poisoning have had a history of having been involved in similar accidents.

This may only occur when accident-prone situations or surroundings are easily accessible to young children.

3. **Location:** The majority of childhood accidental poisonings normally occur in the home. The most common areas for poisoning within the home are the kitchen, bathroom and bedroom. The most common areas for poisoning outside of the home are garage and in automobiles. The highest incidence of accidental poisonings is in the late afternoon and around the dinner hour, or in the early morning hours.

4. **Accessibility:** Accessibility is the principal factor in accidental poisonings in young children. In about 75% of the cases, the materials involved in accidental poisonings have been left within reach of a child.

5. **Type of Container:** The type of container also plays an important role in accidental poisoning. For example, a small quantity of gasoline, solvents in a soft drink bottle, cleaning solution, or paint has been transferred from the original container to a drinking glass or dish.

Important Guidelines To Prevent Accidental Poisoning In Young Children

1. Never refer to medicine as "candy."
2. Do not leave alcohol within a child's reach.
3. Read labels explicitly before administering medications (especially in the middle of the night).
4. Always replace the safety caps as soon as you pour any medicine or use a household substance that can cause injury.
5. Keep the telephone number of your local poison control center by the phone.
6. Teach children never to eat or drink anything that is offered to them by a stranger.
7. Never place inedible products in food containers.
8. Before applying pesticides, remove children, their toys, and pets from the area, and keep them away until the pesticide has dried or as long as is recommended on the label.
9. Be alert for repeat poisonings. Statistics show that children who swallow a poison are likely to attempt it again within a year.

First Aid Treatment For Poisoning

A. General Guidelines

1. If you stay calm then the person you are helping will also stay calm.

2. Protect yourself from poisoning, especially if there is smoke, fumes, or a lot of chemical spilled.

3. Check to see if the person is conscious by talking to them. If you don't get a reply, check that they are breathing and have a pulse. If the person is unconscious, but is breathing and has a pulse, place them on their side (recovery position).

4. If there is no pulse and/or they are not breathing, immediately start resuscitation. The mouth-to-nose technique must be used if there is any chance the rescuer may be contaminated by the poison by using the mouth-to-mouth technique.

5. Call for urgent medical attention, usually an ambulance. Try to identify the chemical or drug involved so that the correct information can be obtained from the National Poison Center.

B. <u>If a poison is swallowed (ingestion)</u>

1. The poisoning (or first aid) advice on containers or packets may not be correct. In all cases where a poison has been swallowed contact the National Poisons Center or a doctor. It is not advisable to make the person vomit. In some cases this may be even dangerous.

2. Giving fluids to drink may not be helpful unless the poison is corrosive, e.g. acid or alkaline. If a corrosive substance is swallowed, give water to drink, and immediately contact the Poison Center for further advice. Have the name of the poison written down when you call.

3. Some household products, such as dishwashing liquids, cause irritation to the stomach leading to nausea and vomiting. It is particularly important in children that if vomiting does occur, none of the vomit is inhaled, as damage to the lungs is possible. Children should not be put to bed after swallowing any poison without first contacting the Poison Center or a doctor.

4. Ipecac should only be given on the advice of the National Poison Center.

C. <u>Splashes in the eye</u>

1. The eyes are very sensitive and are quickly damaged when liquids or powders are splashed into them. Water is recommended for flushing the eyes after exposure to any chemical or product. Flush the eye(s) with copious amounts of water. It is necessary to continue flushing the eye(s) for at least 20 minutes, and sometimes longer. Use a glass or low pressure running water.

2. Always allow the running water to run from the nose to the ear so that the chemical is not flushed into the other eye. While you are flushing, carefully lift the upper and lower lids so that the water can flush away the chemical from under both eyelids. If contact lenses are worn, these should be removed while flushing is in progress.

3. Whenever something is splashed into the eye you should go to the nearest hospital or medical center so that an assessment of the eyes can be made. Do this after you have flushed the eyes. If corrosive products, e.g. acids or alkalis, are splashed in the eye do not hesitate to call an ambulance. Ambulance officers can assist with the flushing while travelling to the hospital. If in doubt always call the National Poison Center, a doctor or ambulance.

D. <u>Smoke, gas and fumes</u>

1. Protect yourself.

2. Remove the person from the source as quickly as possible, making sure they can get plenty of fresh air.

3. Stay upwind of the source.

4. Call for medical assistance from the ambulance service or a doctor.

E. Skin exposure

1. Remove the person from the source of the chemical and immediately flush the affected skin area with copious amounts of water.

2. Remove contaminated clothing and jewelry, unless there is burnt skin or the clothing is stuck to the skin. If a large area of skin has been exposed, call an ambulance while still flushing the affected area. If only a small area is involved, continue flushing with water for 15-20 minutes. If pain, swelling or irritation persists seek medical attention from a hospital or medical center.

3. The Fire Service may be needed to assist with chemical spills. Do not hesitate to call them if you are unsure.

F. Insects and animals

1. If you are bitten or stung, wash the bite with a mild soap and water. Local application of an ice pack may be helpful in reducing pain and swelling. Jellyfish tentacles can be removed by flushing them with sea water or scraping them off with a plastic card.

2. Any open wounds should be treated by a doctor, especially if foreign material is present. If excessive swelling, redness of the skin, itchy hive-like areas, difficulty breathing or swallowing, or a general feeling of illness develops, a doctor should be consulted as soon as possible.

G. Spider bites

1. If possible keep the spider for positive identification. Wash the bite area with a mild soap and water. Apply an ice pack over the area to help relieve pain and swelling if they occur. If signs of infection develop, i.e. redness, swelling, or tenderness, medical attention should be sought.

2. Signs of generalized illness such as abdominal pain, or localized sweating around the bite area, may indicate a serious bite and urgent medical attention should be sought.

ANTIDOTES

Activated charcoal is classified as an effective, nonspecific antidote. It absorbs a large number of materials. Below is the list of drugs/poisons and their antidotes.

	Drugs	Antidotes
1.	Heparin	Protamine
2.	Benzodiazepine	Flumazenil
3.	Beta blocker	Epinephrine, glucagon
4.	Ca-channel blocker	Glucagon, calcium chloride
5.	Digoxin	Digoxin-specific Fab antibody
6.	Potassium	Calcium chloride, sodium bicarbonate, sodium polystyrene sulfonate, glucose and insulin
7.	Acetaminophen	N-Acetylcysteine
8.	Anticholinergic	Physostigmine
9.	Organophosphorus (insecticides)	Atropine
10.	Neostigmine	Atropine
11.	Pyridostigmine	Atropine
12.	Bromide	Sodium or ammonium chloride
13.	Cyanide	Amyl nitrite
14.	Fluoride	Calcium gluconate or lactate
15.	Ethylene glycol	Ethanol
16.	Methanol	Ethanol
17.	Gold	Dimercaprol
18.	Heavy metals	Dimercaprol
19.	Copper	Penicillamine
20.	Lead	Penicillamine
21.	Mercury	Penicillamine
22.	Iron	Deferoxamine
23.	Isoniazid	Pyridoxine
24.	Phenothiazine	Diphenhydramine
25.	Warfarin	Vitamin K (Phytonadione)
26.	Tricyclic antidepressant	Physostigmine
27.	Narcotic analgesic	Naloxone, Naltrexone
28.	Salicylate	Alkaline diuresis
29.	Lithium	Sodium polystyrene sulfonate
30.	Nitrites	Methylene blue
31.	Nitrobenzene	Methylene blue
32.	Chlorates	Methylene blue

U.S Healthcare Delivery System

39. U.S Healthcare System

Ambulatory Care: It is defined as different types of health-related services provided to patients for which they are not required to stay overnight or be hospitalized. For example: outpatients' services provided by physicians.

In The U.S., Ambulatory Care Services Are Provided By:

1. Hospital Outpatient Centers
2. Community Health Centers
3. Ambulatory Surgery Centers
4. Hospital Emergency Departments
5. Free Standing Emergency Centers
6. Family Planning Centers
7. Clinical Laboratory Services
8. Voluntary Health Services
9. Hospitals
10. Long-term Care Services
11. Nursing Homes Services
12. Rehabilitation Facilities
13. Home Health Care
14. Adult Day Care
15. Hospice Care

1. **Hospital Outpatient Centers**: This type of ambulatory care service is normally provided by hospitals. Patients with non-urgent medical problems may visit these types of clinics.

Clinics are normally separated from hospital emergency departments. They may be classified as general or specific according to their specialization. For example, a diabetic clinic center, oncology clinic center, etc.

Hospitals are expanding clinics in the area away from hospitals in order to better serve the community and earn an extra income. There is also another incentive for hospitals to expand the clinic-they can build up a relationship with patients and encourage them to use a clinic's own hospitals for other major medical problems.

2. **Community Health Centers:** Community health centers began to develop in the late 1960s. Initially, funding for these centers was received from the office of economic opportunity and later from U.S. Department of Health, Education and Welfare.

Community centers provide health-related services to a defined population of poor people. Before the existence of community health centers, the poor people and low income patients received healthcare from health departments and hospitals. However, in order to receive help, patients had to wait in a line for hours. To overcome these problems and to provide better health-related services to the poor and needy people, community health centers were developed by the U.S. Department of Health, Education and Welfare.

3. **Ambulatory Surgery Centers:** Due to advancement in healthcare technology and new reimbursement patterns from third parties payers, there has been an increased in the number of outpatient surgeries. In old days, the surgery that may require a stay in the hospital for at least 2 to 3 days, has now been replaced by a same day discharge. This may significantly help the cost-cutting strategy of current health care by avoiding unnecessary hospitalization.

In 1999, there were over 2700 freestanding outpatient surgery centers, up from 2400 in 1996. In addition, Medicare now also covers many outpatient surgeries which may help outpatient surgery centers to compete against hospitals, and cut down unnecessary hospitalization costs.

4. **Hospital Emergency Departments**: The Emergency Room (ER) or Emergency Department (ED) is the most commonly used setting for emergency care. In 1986, the federal government passed an "antidumping law," which indicates that hospitals cannot inquire about the patient's insurance status before providing emergency medical services.

However, this causes a major problem to ERs since most managed care organizations refuse to pay for emergency care without prior authorization. Also, most patients receive emergency medical care either insured or uninsured; this will increase the financial burden on hospitals.

The emergency room is often described under outpatient services since most patients receive the emergency care and are discharged on the same day.

5. **Freestanding Emergency Centers**: Freestanding emergency centers are often as urgicare centers. They provide episodic emergency care 24 hours a day for non-life threatening conditions.

They provide most care on a "walk-in" or appointment basis. Unlike medical clinics, they require payment at the time of service provided. Most of them do not use insurance companies for reimbursements. The form of payment could be check, cash, or credit card. However, they provide complete documentation about services provided to patient to submit to insurance companies in order to receive reimbursement after payment is made to the center.

6. **Family Planning Centers:** It was first established in 1970 when Congress passed Title X of the Public Health Service Act. Under this title, the federal government provides all funding to establish family planning centers. Family planning centers provide a wide range of services which include:

1. Gynecological examinations
2. Breast or cervical screenings
3. Contraceptive information and supplies
4. Routine child health screenings
5. Sexually transmitted disease diagnosis and treatment

7. **Clinical Laboratory Services:** They provide a variety of laboratory analysis to physicians. Most times, physicians collect and send to a nearby clinical laboratory run by a licensed pathologist. In some instances, physicians may send patients to the lab.

Under the 1988 Clinical Laboratory Improvement Amendment Act, all clinical laboratories are required to ensure the quality of test results.

8. **Voluntary Health Agencies**: There are many voluntary health agencies which provide ambulatory care services to patients. These agencies are focused to treat specific diseases and are funded largely by charity. Examples of such agencies are:

A. American Heart Association
B. American Diabetic Association

The services provided by these agencies are not limited to healthcare; they often support research, arrange education programs to increase awareness of patients, and also finance health-needed services.

9. **Hospitals:** Hospitals are considered as the place where patients with acute or severe illnesses may receive medical care. It is a place where patients have access to all medical field specialists, such as physicians, pathologists, nurses, pharmacists, radiologists, and anesthetics. Generally, a hospital is classified in terms of the physical makeup and quantitative nature of services provided.

Hospitals are classified by:

1. Ownership
2. Length of Stay
3. Type of Service
4. Bed Capacity

1. **Ownership Hospitals**: Depending on the ownership of the hospital, it can be subdivided into three major categories:

A. Nonprofit hospitals
B. For profit hospitals
C. Government hospitals

A. **Nonprofit Hospitals**: These are types of hospitals where profits earned by hospitals must be invested back into the hospital's operation or community welfare. They have a board of trustees who voluntarily participate to run and operate hospitals without receiving any pay.

They are exempt from tax requirements. However, in order to qualify for tax-exempt, hospitals must obey a certain criteria provided by federal statutes such as hospitals may not refuse to provide medical care to patients who are unable to pay a fee for service. Most church-affiliated hospitals fall into this category.

B. **For Profit Hospitals:** Unlike nonprofit hospitals, these hospitals operate with the goal of making a profit. The profit earned by these hospitals is distributed to their shareholders who elect the board of directors to operate the hospital.

Due to peer pressure from shareholders and owners, for profit hospitals operate more efficiently with strict cost effectiveness. Therefore, many times for profit hospitals are criticized for paying more attention to cost-cutting strategy than to quality of care.

C. **Government Hospitals:** These types of hospitals are owned and operated by federal governments. These include 27 hospitals for the Army, 19 for the Navy, 44 for the Airforce, and 144 for veterans.

2. **Length of Stay:** Depending on length of stay of a patient, a hospital can be divided into two different categories:

1. Short-Term Hospitals
2. Long-Term Hospitals

Short-Term Hospitals: The average length of stay is less than 30 days.
Long-Term Hospitals: The average length of stay is more than 30 days.

3. **Types of Services:** Depending on types of services, a hospital can be divided into two subcategories:

1. General hospital
2. Special hospital (Cancer, Psychiatric or Pediatric)

4. **Bed Capacity:** Hospitals are also classified according to their bed capacity.

1. Under 50 beds
2. 50-99 beds
3. 100-199 beds
4. 200-299 beds
5. 300-399 beds
6. 400-499 beds
7. 500 beds and over

10. **Long-Term Care Services:** As the name suggests, it offers health-related services to patients for an extended period of time. The members of long-term care are mostly patients of any age with conditions such as birth defects, spinal cord injuries, mental impairments, or any other chronic conditions that may affect a patient's ability to perform normal routine tasks.

However, the majority of long-term patients are elderly. The health related services associated with long-term care are very expensive. Facilities that provide long-term care can be subdivided into two major categories:

A. Nursing Homes Services
B. Rehabilitation Facilities

11. **Nursing Homes**: They represent the large majority of long-term health care. The federal government divides nursing homes into two major categories:

I. A Skilled Nursing Facility (SNF)
II. An Intermediate Care Facility (ICF)

I. **Skilled Nursing Facility (SNF):** It is a nursing home that has been certified as meeting federal standards within the meaning of the Social Security Act. It provides 24-hour nursing home services with medical care which is equivalent to hospitals. The members of SNFs are patients who are suffering from long-term illnesses. In a recent year, a number of hospitals have their own skill nursing units. These will facilitate hospitals to use their acute care beds more efficiently. Hospital-based nursing homes provide better health related services due to their sufficient staffing.

II. **Intermediate Care Facility (ICF):** It is also a nursing home that has been certified as meeting federal standards within the meaning of the Social Security Act. They provide less extensive health related services to patients compared to SNFs.

They have regular nursing services; however it is not 24-hour. The members of ICFs include patients who are not capable of living on their own, yet are not necessarily ill enough to need 24 hour nursing care.

Reimbursement For Nursing Home Services

The cost to cover nursing home care has been increased dramatically. An average premium to obtain or qualify for long-term care services ranges from $400 to $4000 per year depending on the medical condition of patients.

Unfortunately, many patients cannot afford these high premium rates, and consequently rely on Medicare, Medicaid or state or federal grant programs for services.

Even though Medicare does not cover nursing home related services, if a patient is required to obtain services, he should chose an intermediate care facility in order to get reimbursement from Medicare. Since the majorities of patients require intermediate care services rather than extended (skilled) nursing services, Medicare is more favorable to intermediate care facilities when the time comes to pay for the reimbursement.

Prior to 1997, skilled nursing homes were reimbursed by Medicare on the basis of cost plus a margin of profit. However, after the Balance Budget Act of 1997, Medicare has started to pay nursing homes on the basis of flat rate per day. Due to this, many nursing homes are currently facing financial problems, and consequently giving poor medical care.

Unlike Medicare, Medicaid reimburses both SNFs and ICFs. However, patients must reside below the poverty line in order to receive coverage.

The eligibility and coverage for SNFs and ICFs under Medicaid plans depends on the states and may vary greatly. Since Medicaid only covers health-related services if the patient has a very low income, many elderly uses the strategy of "spending down," which involves paying out of pocket until a person becomes poor enough to qualify for Medicaid benefits.

Some elderly also transfer their assets to relatives or trustees in order to protect their assets from Medicaid spending-down provisions.

The Eden Alternative

It was a concept first proposed by Dr. William Thomas. According to him, the elderly faces three major obstacles:

1. Loneliness
2. Helplessness
3. Boredom

Providing solutions for these three obstacles may increase the responsiveness that often cannot be achieved by pills or other therapeutic services. By using this concept, an assisted living facility and community based care services are evolved.

1. **Assisted Living Facilities**: Through the inspiration of Dr. Thomas concept of the "Eden Alternative," care providers have come up with assisted living facilities. They are another alternative to providing care to the elderly who cannot live independently but do not require skilled nursing care.

   Most assisted living facilities now provide an option of an independent residency in an apartment like setting with other facilities such as group meals, laundry, cleaning services, and medication monitoring. The cost associated with assisted living facilities are not covered by any insurance companies. Residents have to make their payments out of their own pocket.

2. **Community Based Care:** Many of the elderly would prefer not to go to nursing homes if the same level of healthcare is provided in the community. However, the current fee structure encourages the elderly to go to nursing homes since Medicare does not cover costs related to community based care centers but pays for nursing homes.

12. **Rehabilitation Facilities:** They provide residential care to patients suffering from traumatic brain injury, strokes, cognitive disorders, and any other problems that may cause permanent disabilities.

    Services include nursing care, physical therapy, occupational therapy, speech therapy and personal care. Their primary goal is to provide the highest level of care to admitted patients so that they can rejoin the community or slow down the progression of disease as much as possible.

    The term "rehabilitation" also applies to mental health and substance abuse organizations.

13. **Home Health Care**: They provide care for the disabled in the community. They provide a vast range of services which include part-time skilled nursing care, physical therapy, speech therapy, occupational therapy, medical social services, medical supplies and equipment-related services.

    The social service such as the bathing and dressing of patients, changing bed linen, and cooking are also provided by home healthcare centers. The costs related to home healthcare services are covered by Medicare, and Medicaid, a small portion is covered by third party insurance companies, and the rest is out of pocket.

14. **Adult Day Care**: It is another form of long-term care service that offers the elderly the chance to remain in the community. They help improve client's overall functioning, and also increase social interaction. They are different from a senior center in that they serve adults who are physically impaired or mentally confused and require supervision.

15. **Hospice Care**: Hospice care provides palliative care and the psychological support needed by terminally ill patients near the end of their lives. They challenge traditional hospital care that often isolates patients at the time when they most need support.

    Patients residing in hospice are allowed to meet their friends and families at all times. They can wear their own choice of clothes and eat meals to their liking with very few restrictions.

    The hospital staff spends unlimited time with patients and delivers more spiritual and emotional care than regular medical care. Medicare covers costs related to hospice services but only for Medicare certified hospices.

40. Important Terminology and Definitions

Acute Care: It is defined as medical care of a limited duration, provided in a hospital or outpatient setting, to treat an injury or short-term illness.

Capitation: A prospective form of reimbursement in which a pharmacy receives a specific amount of money each month for each patient who is eligible to receive a prescription regardless of the service provided. For example, RX Care Pharmacy will receive $100 per month per enrollee of an HMO regardless of services provided to its enrollees.

Catastrophic Coverage: A type of insurance that pays for high-cost health care, usually associated with accidents and chronic illnesses and diseases, such as cancer and AIDS.

Center For Medicare And Medicaid Services (CMS): Administers Medicare, Medicaid, and the Child Health Insurance Programs. Formerly known as the Health Care Financing Administration (HCFA).

Chronic Care: Treatment or rehabilitative health services provided to individuals on a long-term basis (over 30 days), in both inpatient and ambulatory settings.

Coinsurance: It is one type of cost sharing plan in which patients pay a specified percentage (usually 20%) of all losses incurred. For example, if outpatient surgery costs $1000 to a patient and he/she has an 80/20 coinsurance plan, a predetermined amount (20%) of the total costs ($200) should be paid by the patient, and the rest ($800) will be paid by an insurance company.

Consolidated Omnibus Budget Reconciliation Act Of 1985 (COBRA): A federal law that requires that all employer-sponsored health plans to offer certain employees and their families the opportunity to continue, at their persona expense, health insurance coverage under the group plan for up to 18, 24, or 36 months, depending on the qualifying event, after it would have ceased due to the death or retirement of the employee, divorce or legal separation, resignation or termination of employment, or bankruptcy of the employer.

Co-Payment: It is one type of cost-sharing plan in which the patient has to pay a fixed amount each time a service is provided. (e.g. $15 for a physician's visit).

Cost-Sharing: A provision that requires individuals to cover some part of their medical expenses (e.g. copayments, coinsurance, deductibles).

Deductible: It is one type of cost sharing plan in which a patient has to pay a specified amount during a specific period of time (usually one calendar year) before benefits are paid by a third party. For example, if a patient has an insurance plan with a $500 annual deductible and an 80/20 fee structure, and his outpatient surgery costs $1000, then according to the plan, the patient has to first pay $500 (for the given year-one time only) out of his own pocket and the rest ($500) will be shared on the basis of an 80/20 fee structure.

Total Outpatient Surgery Cost	$1000
Patient will pay a one-time deductible for the fiscal year	$500
80% of rest ($500) will be paid by insurance	$400
20% of rest ($500) will be paid by a patient	$100
Total Reimbursement	$1000

Now, let's assume that the same patient within the same fiscal year is admitted to a hospital for another surgery which costs about $3000. This time the patient is not required to pay the $500 deductible since it was in the same fiscal year. Therefore, this time the fee structure would be:

Total Surgery Cost	$ 3000
Patients will pay a one-time deductible for the fiscal year	$ 0.00
80% of ($3000) will be paid by insurance	$ 2400
20% of ($3000) will be paid by a patient	$ 600
Total Reimbursement	$ 3000

Fee Schedule: A listing of accepted fees or established allowances for specified medical procedures as used in health plans; it usually represents the maximum amount the program will pay for the specified procedures.

Diagnosis Related Groups (DRGS): A prospective payment system that pays a set amount for a given diagnosis. If the treatment actually costs less, the provider keeps the excess; if the treatment costs more, the provider loses.

Disproportionate Share Hospital (DSH): A hospital that provides a large amount of uncompensated care and/or care to Medicaid and low-income Medicaid beneficiaries.

Employment Retirement Income Security Act (ERISA): Employee Retirement Income Security Act of 1974. ERISA is the basic law designed to protect the rights of beneficiaries of employee benefit plans offered by employers.

Federal Employee Health Benefit Program (FEHBP): It is also known as the Federal Employee Plan or FEP. The health plans are made available to federal employees as part of their employment benefits.

Fee-For-Service: A billing system in which a healthcare provider charges a patient a set amount for a specific service.

Formulary: A listing of drugs, prepared by The Pharmacy & Therapeutic Committee of a hospital or a managed care company, that may be prescribed by a physician or dispensed by a pharmacist. The physician and pharmacist are requested to use only formulary drugs unless there is a valid medical reason to use non-formulary drugs.

Group Model HMO: An HMO that contracts with a single or multi group of physicians and hospitals to provide health-related services to their plan members. There are two kinds of group model HMOs.

The first type of group model is called the closed panel, in which medical services are delivered in the HMO-owned health center or satellite clinic by physicians who belong to a specially formed but legally separate medical group that only serves the HMO. The group is paid a negotiated monthly capitation fee by the HMO, and the physicians in turn are salaried and generally prohibited from carrying on any fee-for-service practice.

In the second type of group model, the HMO contracts with an existing, independent group of physicians to deliver medical care. Usually, an existing multispecialty group practice adds a prepaid component to its fee-for-service mode and affiliates with or forms an HMO. Medical services are delivered at the group's clinic facilities (both to fee-for-service patients and to prepaid HMO members). The group may contract with more than one HMO.

Group Practices: Three or more physicians who deliver patient care, make joint use of equipments and personnel, and divide income by a prearranged formula.

Health Care Financing Administration (HCFA): The agency of the U.S. Department of Health and Human Services that is responsible for administering the Medicare and Medicaid programs. Now it is known as the Center for Medicaid and Medicare Services (CMS).

Health Maintenance Organization (HMO): Health Maintenance Organization is a healthcare payment and delivery system involving networks of doctors and healthcare institutions. It offers consumers a comprehensive range of benefits at one annual fee (often with copayments or deductibles that vary from service to service) but they can see only providers in the network. Physicians and other health professionals are often on salary or contract with the HMO to provide services. Patients are assigned to a primary care doctor or nurse as a "gatekeeper" who decides what health services are needed and when.

Indemnity Insurance: Benefits are paid in a predetermined amount in the event of a covered loss; differs with reimbursement, which provides benefits based upon actual expenses incurred.

Integrated Delivery System (IDS): A group of healthcare organizations that collectively provides a full range of health-related services in a coordinated fashion to those using the system.

Joint Commission On Accreditation Of Healthcare Organizations (JCAHO): The Joint Commission on Accreditation of Healthcare Organizations, whose mission is to continuously improve the safety and quality of care provided to the public through the provision of healthcare accreditation and related services that support performance improvement in healthcare organizations. Its main purpose is to encourage the attainment of uniformly high standards of institutional medical care. It also establishes guidelines for the operation of hospitals and other health facilities and conducts survey and accreditation programs.

Long-Term Care: A general term for a range of services provided to the chronically ill, physically disabled, and mentally disabled patients in a nursing home or long-term home health care setting.

Managed Care: A system of healthcare delivery that influences or controls utilization of services and costs of services.

Medicaid: A federally aided, state-operated and administered program which provides medical benefits for certain indigent or low-income persons in need of health and medical care. The program, authorized by Title XIX of the Social Security Act, is basically for the poor. It does not cover all of the poor, however, but only persons who meet specified eligibility criteria. Subject to broad federal guidelines, states determine the benefits covered, program eligibility, rates of payment for providers, and methods of administering the program.

Medical Savings Account (MSA): An account similar to an individual retirement account (IRA) into which employers and employees can make tax-deferred contributions and from which employees may withdraw funds to pay covered healthcare expenses.

Medicare: It is Title XVIII of the Social Security Amendment of 1965. The primary health insurance program for people age 65 or older and individual with certain disabilities. Medicare coverage provides acute hospital care, physician services, brief stays in skilled nursing facilities, and short-term skilled home care related to a medical problem. Medicare coverage is determined by the nature of services required by the patient, not the specific diagnosis. Coverage is restricted to medical care, and does not include prescription drugs or custodial care at home or in nursing homes. It is comprised of two major programs:

Hospital Insurance (Part A) and Supplementary Medical Insurance (Part B). The Medicare coverage for Part A has no premium and will pay 100% of a patient's hospital costs for the first 60 days after he/she has paid a deductible of about $720. Medicare Part B pays up to 80% of the patient's doctor bills for a monthly premium of about $50.

Medicare Plus: This Medicare plan gives the option to beneficiaries to choose any plan available where they live, to include fee-for-service (FFS), coordinated care through HMOs, PPOs, POS plans, and PSNs, and a $6000 deductible plan with a medical savings account, union or association plans.

Medicare + Choice: Medicare Part C, formerly known as "Medicare+Choice," is now known as "Medicare Advantage." The introduction of the Medicare+Choice program represents what is arguably the most significant change in the Medicare program since its inception in 1965. As its name implies, the primary goal of the Medicare + Choice program is to provide Medicare beneficiaries with a wider range of health plan choices to complement the original Medicare option. Alternatives available to beneficiaries under the Medicare+Choice program include both the traditional managed care plans (such as HMOs) that have participated in Medicare on a capitated payment, as well as a broader range of plans comparable to those now available through private insurance.

Medigap: It is also known as Medicare Supplement Insurance, a type of private insurance coverage that may be purchased by an individual enrolled in Medicare to cover certain needed services that are not covered by Medicare Parts A and B.

Morbidity: An episode of sickness, as defined by a health professional. A morbidity rate is the number of such episodes occurring in a given population during a given period of time.

Mortality: A death. A mortality rate is the number of deaths occurring during a given period of time.

Natality: A live birth. The natality rate is the number of live births occurring in a given population during a given period of time.

Per Diem Payment: An amount a payor will pay for one day of care, which includes all hospital charges associated with the inpatient day (including nursing care, surgeries, medications, etc.).

Point-Of-Service Plan (POS): A type of managed care plan combining features of health maintenance organizations (HMOs) and preferred provider organizations (PPOs). A patient can decide whether to go to a network provider and pay a flat amount or to an out-of-network provider and pay a deductible and/or a coinsurance charge.

Preferred Provider Organization (PPO or PPA): A Preferred Provider Organization (PPO) provides a list of contracted "preferred" providers from which to choose. Patients receive the highest monetary benefit when they limit their healthcare services to those providers on the list. If they go to a doctor or hospital that is not on the preferred provider list referred to as going "out-of-network," then the plan covers a smaller percentage of their healthcare expenses or may cover none of their healthcare expenses based on the contract wording of the plan.

Quality Assurance: A formal set of activities to measure the quality of service provided; these may also include corrective measures.

Reinsurance: Insurance purchased by a health plan to protect it against extremely high cost cases.

Staff Model HMO: An HMO that employs providers directly and those providers see members in the HMO's own facilities; a kind of closed panel HMO.

Account Receivable Collection Period: The amount of time between when the sale is made and the cash is collected.

Goodwill: Benefits to a pharmacy arising out of its reputation, continued patronage, favorable location and similar intangible advantages.

Intangible Assets: Assets which are of value to the pharmacy and which may produce income but do not have a readily determinable value, e.g. Goodwill

Tangible Assets: Touchable assets which have physical form and qualities, e.g. inventory, fixtures, etc.

AAC (Actual Acquisition Cost): The actual price paid by a pharmacy after all trade, volume and cash discounts.

AWP (Average Wholesale Price): The published "list price" of a particular drug product.

EAC (Estimated Acquisition Cost): The third party's estimate of the price paid by pharmacies for a particular drug product.

MAC (Maximum Allowable Cost): The maximum amount that will be paid by a third party to a pharmacy for a particular product.

Acquisition Cost: The cost at which a product is acquired from a direct or indirect source; it includes all discounts except the cash discount.

Cost of Dispensing: The sum of all direct expenses, indirect expenses and losses due to reductions. When the cost of dispensing is be related to a specific professional fee, this sum is divided by the estimated number of prescriptions to be dispensed.

Elasticity of Demand: A measure of the extent to which the sale of quantities of a product will change in response to a change in price or other merchandising variable.

Direct Expenses: Operating costs that occur for a department only because it exists.

Indirect Expenses: All facilitating operating costs generated by the business for the benefit of its department; overhead expenses.

Variable Expenses: Operating costs which increase or decrease directly with sales volume change, however not always to the same degree.

Differential Analysis: The process of estimating the consequences of alternative actions that decision-makers take. Differential costs are the costs that increase when taking a particular course of action. Differential revenue is the additional revenue that accrues by taking a particular course of action.

Drug Utilization Review (DUR): It is the type of study that is conducted by health plan sponsors to monitor the frequency and usage of prescription drugs. The review can range from assessing the number of prescriptions per member per month, to an evaluation of compliance with therapeutic guidelines. A review of paid claims is called "retrospective DUR," a review conducted at the time of prescription dispensing is known as "concurrent DUR", and a review that is conducted prior to dispensing the prescription is known as "prospective DUR."

Earned Discount: The difference between AWP and AAC is known by earned discount. This discount is normally greater for pharmacies that buy in larger volume and have more efficient purchasing practices.

Exclusive Provider Arrangement (EPA): A managed health care system that limits the number of providers that may participate. It is also known as a "closed panel."

Pharmacy Benefit Management (PBM): The company which contracts with the pharmacy and manages the logistical functions of the third party program on behalf of the corporate purchaser of a prescription drug benefit program.

Prospective Reimbursement: A form of reimbursement in which a pharmacy is paid in advance an amount estimated to cover prescriptions that will be dispensed to plan beneficiaries later. There are several payment methods that fall under the umbrella of PPS: DRGs (inpatient admissions); APCs (outpatient visits); RBRVS (professional services); and RUGs (skilled nursing home care).

Retrospective Reimbursement: A form of reimbursement in which the pharmacy is paid after submitting a claim for a prescription dispensed to a plan beneficiary. Also called "Fee-For-Service."

Adjusted Average Per Capita Cost (AAPCC): It is normally used by the Health Care Financing Administration as the calculation for funds required caring for Medicare recipients. The risk contract reimbursement is 95% of the AAPCC fee-for-service expenditures on a 5 year rolling average for a county.

Agency For Healthcare Policy And Research (AHCPR): It was created by congress in 1989 under Public Law 101-239 as a public health service agency to collect and share information to improve healthcare delivery.

Capitated Payment: A contractually agreed fee (monthly, bimonthly, or annual) paid by an HMO or CMP to either an IDN, hospital, physician, or group practice, in exchange for healthcare services to enrolled members.

Case Mix: The manner of describing the tendency of group of covered lives to utilize services; in terms of the frequency and intensity of hospital admissions or services reflecting different needs and uses of hospital resources. It can be measured based on patient's diagnosis, severity of a patient's illness, the utilization of services, and the characteristics of a hospital. Case mix influences cost and scope of services provided by a hospital.

Health Risk Assessment (HRA): A health promotion or wellness program used to evaluate the health status of a patient or employee, which can either be performed on-site or off-site from the work location, through an automated or written format of questions and answers. Programs may evaluate general health status or may be more targeted toward cardiovascular health, with related risks and recommendations for how to reduce risks.

Medicare Risk Contract: The Medicare Risk Contract program was initially authorized in 1982 to allow Health Maintenance Organizations (HMOs) and similar organizations to contract with Medicare. In return for a per-capita payment, the organization is at full risk for providing medically necessary Medicare services to enrolled beneficiaries. The risk contract program has gradually grown to include 12.5 percent of beneficiaries in mid-1997. Problems with the adjusted average per capita cost and the lack of choices other than HMOs, however, appears to have limited the growth of this program and helped convince Congress to enact changes.

Medical Loss Ratio (MLR): The ratio between the costs to deliver medical care, versus how much revenue is made from premiums. Insurance companies often have a medical loss ratio of 96 percent or more. The tightly managed HMOs may have medical loss ratios of 75 percent to 85 percent. It is a common way to find out the efficiency of a given HMO or health plan.

MLRs have been reduced during the 1990s, from low 90% to the 70% range, but in recent years, they may be swinging back up as profitability is challenged.

Management Service Organization (MSO): An organization that provides practice management, administrative, and support service to individual physicians or group practices. It is also known as Medical Service Organization or a Shared Services Organization (SSO).

Per Member Per Month (PMPM): Applies to a revenue or cost for each enrolled member each month.

National Committee For Quality Assurance (NCQA): The National Committee for Quality Assurance (NCQA) is an independent, non-profit organization dedicated to measuring the quality of America's health care. The organization is governed by a Board of Directors that includes employers, consumer and labor representatives, health plans, quality experts, regulators, and representatives from organized medicine.

Its mission is to improve the quality of healthcare delivered to people everywhere. To achieve this goal, NCQA's efforts are organized around two activities, accreditation and performance measurement (report cards), which are complementary strategies for producing information to guide a patient's choice.

P&T Committee: The main focus of the committee is to develop policy and educate healthcare professionals on various aspects of healthcare-related subjects. As far as development of policy concerns, most policies are related to evaluate and select drugs to be included in the formulary. The P&T committee also develops other policies pertaining to drug therapy to ensure safe and cost-effective drug therapy.

Zero Premium: In some Medicare marketplaces, there is a practice of not charging any added monthly premium (also known as zero premium) to (plan members) what is already paid for coverage of the Part B Medicare program, versus the practice of an HMO getting a monthly premium in addition to what is paid to the federal government by the patient.

Accelerated Death Benefit: A benefit that allows a terminally ill insured to receive part of the face amount of their life insurance policy in advance of their death, as either in one lump sum or in installments.

Psychometrics: The science of measuring the characteristics of human behavior, personality, cognitive abilities, interests, or aptitudes.

Validity: A test is said to be valid if it measures what it claims to measure. There is no single validity coefficient for a test. A test is always valid for some purpose, and therefore is more valid in some circumstances than in others.

Construct Validity: This refers to whether a test is measuring what it claims to measure as judged by accumulated evidence. A variety of statistical techniques can be used to see if the test behaves in ways predicted by the given construct. For example, a new test of computer programming skills would be expected to correlate highly with other valid tests of computer skills. Conversely, this new test would be expected to have little correlation with a different type of test (such as a test of social intelligence).

Concurrent Validity: A test is said to have concurrent validity if it correlates highly with a "benchmark" test of the same variables.

Content Validity: This refers to tests such as skills, ability or attainment tests where the domain of items is much defined. A test with good content validity represents and samples adequately from the curriculum or content domain being tested. This kind of validity involves logical comparisons and judgments by the test developers rather than a specific statistical technique. For example, a high school biology test has content validity if it tests knowledge taken from biology textbooks assigned to students and reinforced by teachers in their instructional program.

Criterion Validity: It is the degree to which a test predicts some criterion (measure of performance), usually in the future. To ascertain this kind of validity, evaluators look at the correlation between the test and the criterion measure. For example, a college admission test has criterion validity if it can predict some aspect of college performance (e.g., grades, degree completion).